The Eye
of the Hurricane

Also of Interest

Modern Germany: A Social, Cultural, and Political History, Henry M. Pachter

Communism and Political Systems in Western Europe, edited by David E. Albright

The Spanish Political System: Franco's Legacy, E. Ramón Arango

Norway, Oil, and Foreign Policy, John C. Ausland

Ideology and Politics: The Socialist Party of France, George A. Codding, Jr., and William Safran

The Netherlands: An Historical and Cultural Survey, 1795–1977, Gerald Newton

Managing Transnationalism in Northern Europe, Bengt Sundelius

Post-War Europe: A Political Geography, Mark Blacksell

About the Book and Author

The Eye of the Hurricane:
Switzerland in World War Two
Urs Schwarz

Despite the voluminous research published about World War II, there has remained a surprising gap; there is little, perhaps nothing, on the role of Switzerland. It was in the neutral Swiss oasis – where a perilous balancing act was required for survival – that a combination of determination and delicate negotiation continued to frustrate the Axis powers.

Urs Schwarz cuts through the myths surrounding this period in a narrative based largely on his experiences as both participant and observer. He was a soldier, then a journalist in war-torn Berlin, and, beginning in 1942, foreign editor of the *Neue Zürcher Zeitung.* These experiences, and subsequent extensive research, result here in a unique and discerning – and colorful – history.

Before World War II, Urs Schwarz studied law at the Universities of Zurich and Berlin and received the Ll.M. degree from Harvard. He founded (1951) and edited the *Swiss Review of World Affairs,* served as associate professor of the Graduate Institute for International Studies, Geneva, and was founding director of the International Press Institute.

The Eye
of the Hurricane

Switzerland
in World War Two

Urs Schwarz

Westview Press / Boulder, Colorado

ENDPAPER MAPS

The endpaper maps show the maximum extent of Axis domination in World War II, in October 1942. In Russia, the Germans had reached the Volga River near Stalingrad; in Africa, Rommel had not yet been defeated at El Alamein; the U.S. landings on the North African coast were not until November 1942; and in the north, the Germans held Finland and Norway. Thus, neutral Sweden was completely encircled.

On the map, the solid lines indicate the front lines reached by the German armies. The dotted lines crossing the seas and linking the land fronts show the sea areas the Germans could more or less dominate, since they possessed the corresponding coasts and all the ports. Only Great Britain and Ireland and the neutral countries Sweden, Spain, and Portugal were outside this sphere. The black area in the middle is, of course, Switzerland.

Copyright © 1980 by Westview Press, Inc.

Published in 1980 in the United States of America by
  Westview Press, Inc.
  5500 Central Avenue
  Boulder, Colorado 80301
  Frederick A. Praeger, Publisher

Library of Congress Cataloging in Publication Data
Schwarz, Urs, 1905–
    The eye of the hurricane: Switzerland in World War Two.
    Includes index.
    1. World War, 1939-1945 – Switzerland. 2. Switzerland – History – 20th century.
I. Title.
D754.S9S37   940.53'494   79-26404
ISBN 0-89158-766-7

Printed and bound in the United States of America

I send you forth as sheep in the midst of wolves:
be therefore wise as serpents.

−St. Matthew 10: 16

Contents

Preface

The wish to set down an account of the extraordinary adventure of Switzerland, caught by the hurricane called World War II and surviving almost miraculously, without actually fighting, suddenly kindled in my mind the time when an American friend of mine (a distinguished scholar, teacher, and philosopher) remarked that in all that had been written about Europe in that period of history there was a blank spot: the small republic in the center of Europe. In the colossal body of literature dealing with the drama of the Second World War, Switzerland is mentioned, of course, but rather incidentally. Since this small country was neutral and seemingly not a protagonist in the conflict, one can understand why Clio did not bother to record events affecting it. Yet they were perhaps more dramatic in their political and psychological complexities than outright fighting in many a battle. In Switzerland, much has been written on this period, but little seems to have made an impact outside its borders.

That expression "blank spot" at once recalled to my mind faces of people I had known and events I had witnessed, all almost forgotten, buried under what has been happening since 1945. I saw myself, involved as a soldier and as a journalist in those events. I recalled nights at the command post of an antiaircraft battery, when British bombers droned over our heads; days on observation posts on the border, when the noise of battle rolled closer and closer; moments in the correspondents' office in Berlin, when the sirens wailed and bombs fell, or at the foreign editor's desk of the *Neue Zürcher*

Zeitung in Zurich, when German attacks seemed imminent. The "blank spot" came alive with faces of people I had known: General Guisan, Chief of Staff Huber, the successive presidents Pilet-Golaz, Minger, Kobelt, the army corps commanders and division commanders Wille, Bircher, Berli, the colonels Däniker, Barbey, Gonard, Masson, the famous Dr. Max Husman; on the German side, Ribbentrop, von Weizsäcker, Köcher, Rahn; among the Americans, Allen Dulles, Dean Acheson, and Leland Harrison, to mention only a few. They beckoned me to write the full story.

Here it is – based on my own experiences, on the wealth of writings dealing both with the whole period and with specific aspects of it, on published treatises, memoirs, documents, as far as they seemed significant, all seen through the eyes of one who was deeply involved.

I also followed Michel de Montaigne's advice: "He who judges surely and healthily uses freely his own experiences as well as things received from others, and he speaks freely of himself, as well as of others."[1]

Of the authors to whom I am most indebted, I wish to mention in this place only a few: Edgar Bonjour with his monumental *Geschichte der schweizerischen Neutralität;* Bernard Barbey with his elegantly indiscreet *P. C. du Général* and *Aller et retour;* Hans Rudolf Kurz, author of a great number of monographs and articles on this period, among them his remarkable *Die Schweiz in der Planung der kriegführenden Mächte;* and René-Henri Wüst, who published in 1966 his excellent *Alerte en pays neutre.* There are many others, whom space prevents me from mentioning, to whom I also owe a debt of gratitude.[2]

It is my hope that some of those who have judged the policies and attitudes of the Swiss government and of the Swiss people on the basis of information available until now, and some of those who have known little about the contribution to history made by a small yet resolved nation placed by the accident of geography in the middle of the struggle, may glance at the present pages. I also would like to think that some scholar or writer, who may plan to write or speak on World War II but did not have the opportunity to live through the events as they unfolded, may find some inspiration in what I have written. I have striven to present the cold facts and at the same time let the reader feel the scorching winds of mortal danger that swept across the borders of Switzerland in those years.

A final, yet deeply felt word of thanks goes to two men without whose contributions I could not have produced this account as it now stands: to Professor Louis J. Halle, Geneva, from whose interest for the *whole* story of World War II the plan of the study originated, and to the late Patrick Smith, O.B.E., an admired colleague in journalism and former correspondent of the BBC, Locarno, who read the manuscript and made invaluable suggestions as to form and contents.

Urs Schwarz

The Eye
of the Hurricane

CHAPTER ONE

Electing the General

The Armed Forces

In the late afternoon of August 30, 1939, the two chambers of the Swiss Parliament meeting in joint session elected (by 202 votes out of a total of 229) Henri Guisan as commander-in-chief of the armed forces. After the vote, the presiding chairman of the National Council, whose mother tongue was French but who at that moment expressed himself in German, wishing to have the newly elected general ushered in, ordered his aides, by a slip of the tongue, "to search for the general." He had literally translated the French word *chercher*, corresponding to "invite, bring in," to the German *suchen*, which means to "look or search for somebody in an unknown place." This caused some hilarity in an otherwise solemn and tense moment.

The new commander-in-chief, whose appointment had been agreed upon shortly after the Munich crisis of 1938, both by the government and the political leaders in Parliament, had, of course, been waiting in the wings. He immediately entered the council chamber, unescorted, and pronounced, in French, the traditional oath of office. At that same instant, he was promoted from the rank of corps commander to the rank of four-star general. (The Swiss military system has only one general, and that only in time of war or serious threats. In peacetime the highest rank is corps commander.)

Henri Guisan, born in 1874, the son of a country doctor in the sturdy peasant environment of the canton of Vaud, had been interested in jurisprudence and theology but finally studied agriculture. He managed a farm of his own, with plenty of time to devote to military duties. As a militia officer he had served in the field artillery and on the general staff with such success that in 1926, he was promoted to division commander. At that point he joined the corps of professional officers.

A wave of enthusiasm swept over the parliamentarians and, beyond the walls of the Federal Palace in Berne, throughout the whole country. The election of this high-ranking officer had been hoped for, and indeed expected. He seemed to represent the best of Swiss military traditions; the elegant silhouette of this horseman was well known throughout the nation. Many thousands who had served under him or had otherwise met him knew his simple ways, his firmness, and his kindness.

The moment was one of solemnity indeed. The constitution and the law confers on the general (once he is elected to his unique rank and position) almost unlimited powers. So sweeping are they that they never have been fully exercised, even by former generals such as Henri Dufour in 1847, 1849, 1856, and 1859, Hans Herzog in 1870, or Ulrich Wille in 1914, but always exercised in a limited way, based on negotiation and compromise between the military and the federal government.[1] In principle, subordination of the military to the civil power was always considered as an axiom of national policy and never questioned. Actually, on that afternoon of August 30, 1939, the two chambers of Parliament had enacted a law giving the government (the Federal Council) full powers for maintaining the security, independence, and neutrality of Switzerland, for defending the economic interests of the country, and for insuring its economic survival.

Notwithstanding, the election of the general carried this simple message to every Swiss man and woman, even to those ignorant of the full constitutional and legal significance of the act: We are entering upon a time of crisis, perhaps war. The army will be mobilized. Life "as usual" is at an end. Strenuous testing times of sacrifice and unknown dangers are upon us.

The previous day, the federal government had ordered the mobilization of the forces for the immediate protection of the national borders. Frontier guard units had been formed by men living in localities near the frontier – regular army soldiers with full military training and instruction. Within hours they had occupied the lightly armed fortifications commanding the accesses toward the interior of the country, had installed the explosive charges necessary to blow up bridges and narrow passages of strategic importance for an attacker, had set up barbed-wire obstacles, and had laid minefields in critical sectors. At the same time the entire personnel of the air force and the antiaircraft artillery had reported for duty to the various air bases. However weak, the air force was combat-ready within hours. It included, at that time, about 150 Swiss-built airplanes of doubtful military value and 50 excellent German Messerschmitt Me-109 fighter planes.

On September 1, when it was known that Germany and the Soviet Union had invaded Poland without declaration of war, the new commander-in-chief went before the federal government and requested the general mobilization of the army. It was ordered the same day. When at noon on September 3, 1939, the United Kingdom declared war on the German Reich and the Second World War was on, the army was ready in its assigned sectors: 435,000 men, grouped in three army corps and assorted specialized units, were ready to move into the positions that would be dictated by the developing war beyond the frontiers. It was an impressive force considering the small total population of 4.2 million at that time.[2]

The traditional policy of neutrality necessitated total military preparedness. Accordingly the forces, once mobilized, were deployed to meet threats from any direction imaginable. The main concentrations of troops were directed toward the northeast and northwest. In these sectors the country was most vulnerable, and the military threat in case of a war between Germany and France was most serious. The task of the forces deployed in these directions was to prevent either the German or the French army from invading Swiss territory in an attempt to outflank the fortifications confronting one another across the Rhine River north of Basel. In ad-

dition to this, three fortified areas barred access to the strategically important alpine passes. Other forces faced west,
south, and east.

The Spirit of 1939

The rise of National Socialism in Germany had been
viewed by the vast majority of the Swiss population as a
disaster, both for Germany and for the world. The events of
1934, when Hitler ordered the assassination of his potential
opponents on the right and the left, had revealed the criminal
character of Hitler's regime. It was openly denounced as such
by the Swiss press. In the German-speaking part of Switzerland, where the people could and usually did listen on the
radio to the incredibly violent Sunday speeches of the Führer,
he was viewed as a reckless demagogue, both dangerous and
ridiculous. The monster rallies of National Socialism seemed
both ludicrous and disgusting to the sober and thoroughly
democratic Swiss. The age-old and innate Swiss dislike of the
Germans, of their language, their verbosity, and their arrogance, was never far below the surface in spite of close
business, cultural, and family connections, and it now came
out into the open. This dislike was gradually transformed into
a fundamental hatred by the spectacles of German reckless-
ness and the antics of the National Socialist leaders and their
brown hordes.

It was not surprising that in the French-speaking areas of
Switzerland, where most people could not understand all this
neo-German jargon, it took much longer to open people's eyes
to the real character of National Socialism. In this part of the
Swiss Confederation interest centers around France – in the
press of Geneva, Lausanne, and Neuchâtel, for example,
local events in Paris are reported like other local events
nearer home – and there is practically no family or business
relationship with what is commonly considered as the bar-
barian country to the north, so the new German political
system did not arouse much interest. For a long time many
Suisses romands believed that Hitler was a conservative force
of order and a bulwark against Communism.

The anti–National Socialist and anti-German feeling of the overwhelming majority of the Swiss found powerful expression in the press – and also on the tiny stages of some popular cabarets. The state-controlled German press reacted strongly and never tired of ridiculing Switzerland for being small and politically backward, for its lack of understanding of true greatness as represented by the German Reich and its Führer, and for its lack of interest in the brilliant New Order, which Hitler was preparing for the whole of Europe, etc.

The invasion and annexation of Austria on March 11, 1938, an inglorious end to the independence of a small neighboring country, had come as a deep shock to the Swiss. They understood that Austria had been undermined by the National Socialist propaganda so that the country fell without firing a shot, without even a token sign of resistance. They also understood that the antidemocratic movements that had evolved within Switzerland in recent years were trying to prepare a similar fate for their own country. These movements, inspired from Italy and Germany as everybody knew, were small in size yet great in arrogance.

The dismemberment of Czechoslovakia in March 1939 by the application of German threats, aided and abetted by the cowardly passivity of the European powers, generated a deep apprehension and a desperate resolve in wide sections of the Swiss population to resist a similar fate.

The military attack against Poland in September 1939, and the defeat of a nation that traditionally enjoyed sympathy in the alpine republic and that had been considered as a model of military strength, came as a new shock. Could any one now doubt, after these precedents, that the German war machine would soon turn against other neighboring countries, especially against a country so provocative to the German tyrant and his advisers because it was democratic, small, in part German-speaking, and had a press that never hid its dislike for the new Germany and its hatred for National Socialism, and even ridiculed the great Führer himself? Some German publications had openly advocated the inclusion of at least the German-speaking parts of Switzerland in the *Grossdeutsche Reich* – the rest might go to Italy and to France.

Subversive groups in Switzerland, as we shall see, openly propagated a similar program.

Pro-German Movements and Subversion

As early as 1923, under the influence of the triumph of Fascism in Italy, antidemocratic movements had begun to evolve in Switzerland.[3] They were a mixture of different ingredients, had divergent ideological trends, and sprang from many roots. First of all, the spirit of imitation is always alive in Switzerland, perhaps due to its smallness and a longing for national splendor by people frustrated by the diminutive size of their own country. One finds conservative elements basically critical of the liberal, Masonic, and anticlerical roots of the Swiss Conferation as founded in 1848, together with advocates of the Roman Catholic vision of a corporative state, perhaps combined too with some lingering anti-Semitism. Then there is hatred of the bourgeoisie and of big business, the quest for greater social equality as well as a deep dislike of Communism as developed in the Soviet Union. There are those who naively thought National Socialism a bulwark against Communism. There were also the romantic admirers of the heroic military traditions of the Swiss nation who did not believe in neutrality. Members of the lunatic fringe joined hands with misled patriots, well-meaning critics of real national weaknesses associated themselves with frustrated unsuccessful people rejected by the closely knit, tradition-bound Swiss society. The economic crisis of the thirties, with many unemployed or underpaid, added its share of discontented people from the working class.

At least a dozen organizations were founded—combining, splitting, and quarreling constantly in the course of the years, changing names, and federating again. To list them all would be extremely tedious. The first, and largest, was the National Front, which in costume, terminology, and behavior faithfully copied the German example. The Communist party also, which owed strict allegiance to Moscow, unfolded a frenetic propaganda and attracted many.

A typical illustration of the almost lunatic character of

these movements is found in the tragic fate of a young Swiss, Maurice Bavaud, who attempted to assassinate Hitler on November 9, 1938, was sentenced to death, and was executed in Berlin in 1941. The young man was a fervent Roman Catholic and a passionate anti-Communist, basically antidemocratic, yet was induced by his friends to kill Hitler, whom they found neither anti-Communist nor anti-Semitic enough.[4]

According to the leader of one of these groups, called the *Eidgenössische Soziale Arbeiterpartei*, the number of sympathizers for totalitarian systems of different shades was, in 1939, about forty thousand.[5] In reality it was probably less. The noise, the demonstrations, their quarrels, and their own journals, however, projected the image of a powerful movement. Most writings of a later date reflect this exaggerated view of the influence of these minorities. Since the overwhelming majority, which was unflinchingly patriotic and democratic, did not by far make nearly such a fuss, most writers – serious historians as well as journalist-novelists, television producers as well as moviemakers of our day – have succumbed to the fascination of those arrogant movements.

These pro-Nazi organizations were not large, but they were dangerous; not because they appealed to any significant sector of the Swiss people, but because they were a hotbed in which German propaganda, espionage, and subversion could thrive. Subversion was clearly planned. Students were recruited in Germany to be sent to Switzerland with the task of winning sympathizers among their colleagues. The Germans living in Switzerland were forced by cunning, pressure, propaganda, and open threats to organize themselves along the pattern of the National Socialist German Workers' Party (NSDAP). In Switzerland the party had set up a center which was headed by Wilhelm Gustloff, who behaved among his compatriots as the unchallenged totalitarian leader. On February 5, 1936, he was assassinated by a medical student of the University of Berne, a young man of Yugoslav nationality, David Frankfurter. He said that he sought revenge for the Jews martyred in Germany. In December of the same year Frankfurter was sentenced in the Swiss city of Chur to eighteen years in prison for murder.[6]

The federal government refused to give the party permission to appoint a successor to Gustloff. So it was that the German legation in Berne, under diplomatic cover and a little more discreetly, assumed the same function. To the Swiss police, army, and the public there was no doubt that the Germans had established a network of agents who, in case of a war, would commit acts of sabotage and would be supported by members of the pro–National Socialist groups, such as the National Front.

These organizations became, as we shall see, very active in the moments of greatest danger and discouragement after the defeat of France in 1940. Convinced that the "New Europe" of Hitler's making was just around the corner, they finally amalgamated into one party called the *Nationale Bewegung der Schweiz* (NBS), the National Movement of Switzerland. The federal government, under the prevailing influence of the foreign minister and president for 1940, Marcel Pilet-Golaz, had condoned their almost treasonable activities far too long, out of fear of Germany.

On November 17, 1940, the general sent to the government a report of the intelligence service of the army describing the NBS as endangering the security of the state. In the letter of transmission Guisan added, "These activities inspire serious apprehensions if adequate measures are not taken against them before it is too late."[7] Two days later the Federal Council (government) gathered its courage, dissolved the National Movement and all possible successors, and prohibited its journal. On November 26 the government prohibited the Communist party, which, as then was revealed, was in close contact with the extremists of the right. A sigh of relief went through the whole country, and confidence in the government, which had been severely harmed by the many signs of weakness it had shown throughout the fateful years of 1939 and 1940, began to be restored.

Facing the Blitzkrieg

When World War II broke out in September 1939, the general had been elected, the army mobilized, the Swiss nation – in spite of the antidemocratic movements – was united in its will to remain neutral in the struggle and, if attacked, to fight for its independence and institutions. A national exhibition – a most colorful fair called the *Landesausstellung* or *"Landi"* – was held in Zurich that very year. In those tense months it turned out to be a welcome and powerful reminder for all the people that it was worthwhile to fight for one's country, which had become, under its free and democratic institutions, such a success and an example of progress and order.

Poland was overwhelmed by the German *Wehrmacht*, with the treacherous assistance of the Soviet Union, in just twenty days. The next move of the German war machine and of the German warlord, drunk with his easy success in the east of Europe, certainly would be directed toward the west. General Guisan and his staff, basing their planning on the most recent war experiences in Poland, immediately took the necessary steps to oppose a German attack.

As Switzerland had no mechanized forces at this time and its artillery and air force were only in the initial stages of modernization, salvation could only be attained by stubbornly resisting in a naturally strong position. Wide areas of the country would have to be abandoned. The panzers must be prevented, at all costs, from making their now notorious breakthrough and enveloping movements. The Swiss army knew it had nothing to oppose the panzers once they were free to move in the rear of a pierced position.

The solution chosen by Guisan and the chief of the general staff, Corps Commander Jakob Labhart, was embodied in an order of October 4, 1939. The plan was to hold a main line of resistance with the masses of well-armed infantry available and with the artillery partly deployed as antitank weapons. The position would run along a line of rivers, lakes, and mountain chains providentially disposed parallel to the German border. To make up for the desperate lack of modern artillery, the 120-mm position pieces dating from 1882, which were at that time being replaced by modern guns, were kept in service. Eighty-four-mm pieces from the last century were brought out from the arsenals where they had slept peacefully since 1918. There was no army reserve to speak of. Everything was used to make the one position strong. There were only two alternatives: either the position held or it broke. In the latter event, that would be the end.[8]

This main position was protected by an advanced line of defenses already existing, which closely followed the national border. They had been organized and built from 1934 to 1939 and consisted of a system of blockhouses armed with machine guns, connected in strategic areas by antitank obstacles and minefields. The advanced line also included a number of forts armed with artillery. This thin line, naturally strong because of its favorable terrain, was to prevent a surprise attack and to delay the enemy. It ran through the high Alps in the south and east, then along the river Rhine and through the Jura Mountains to the area of Geneva, excluding the city itself. (The term Jura Mountains designates a number of parallel chains of wooded hills stretching from the area of Schaffhausen westward, running south of Basel and north of Geneva, far into France.)

The main area of resistance, manned and organized from the beginning of October 1939, was marked by a line of rivers, lakes, and chains of mountains or steep, wooded hills which, it was hoped, would be a serious obstacle to the German armored forces. The area began at the fortress of Sargans, which was still under construction, then followed the lakes of Walensee and Zurichsee, the river Limmat, then the chains of the Jura Mountains, and ended at the heights of Gempen overlooking the city of Basel from the south. An exaggerated strategic importance gradually was given to this group of hills, as so often happens in history with places of limited importance. One such example was the disproportionate significance given in the Thirty Years War to the small city of Breisach (on the Rhine, sixty kilometers north of Basel).

Whereas Basel lay ahead of the main area of resistance and was covered only by a strongly fortified advance line, the large city of Zurich was practically included in the main defenses. With its many bridges straddling the river Limmat, it was to form a colossal stronghold—a Stalingrad *avant la lettre*.

The line of defense was manned by six divisions and a task force holding a strategic point west of Zurich. One light brigade was to bar one specific line of advance in the east. The eastern and southern borders were protected by one mountain division and one mountain brigade. One mountain division and one mountain brigade formed a kind of mobile reserve for the whole.

Work on the main line of defense, significantly called the Army Position because practically the whole army was in it, went on throughout the winter 1939/40, during the whole "phony war." The Soviet attack against Finland, launched on November 30, 1939, and the stubborn resistance of the Finns along their Mannerheim Line and in their northern forests against the Russian armored divisions encouraged the Swiss and confirmed their trust in the position they were building up. Hard work – digging trenches and shelters and setting up obstacles – tough training for combat under a strong leadership, and iron discipline prevented the army from becoming bored and demoralized, as happened with the French forces in the Maginot Line and north of it.

Still, having so many men on active service produced problems for the economy of the nation as a whole and for every individual officer and soldier – problems that were soon to be felt during the first cold and gloomy winter of the war. Pressure by political parties and trade unions to allow the men to return to their families and their work was strong throughout the whole *drôle de guerre*, the "phony war." Step by step, troops were demobilized. By December 31, 1939, the number of men under arms had been reduced to 175,000. A system of rotation permitted the men to return home at regular intervals. On December 20, 1939, the government enacted legislation creating a system that protected the soldier against financial losses caused by his active service. He received forthwith an allowance calculated according to the size of his family and the pay earned in civilian life. The cost was divided among the government, the employers, and the employee, who, while he worked, had to contribute 2 percent of his wages. The whole system proved to be a highly successful social measure.

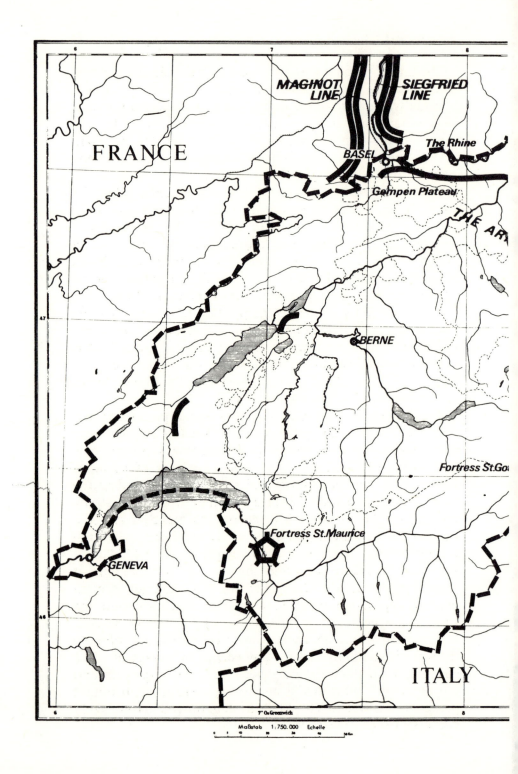

MAGINOT
LINE

SIEGFRIED
LINE

The Rhine

FRANCE

BASEL

Gempen Plateau

THE AR

BERNE

Fortress St.Go

Fortress St.Maurice

GENEVA

ITALY

7° 0s Greenwich

Maßstab   1:750.000   Echelle

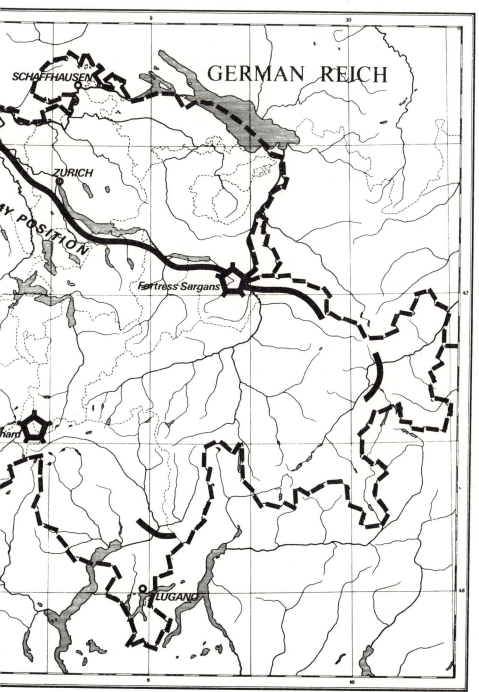

SCHAFFHAUSEN

GERMAN REICH

ZURICH

POSITION

Fortress Sargans

47

hard

46

LUGANO

© Kümmerly & Frey, Geographischer Verlag, Bern

When, on April 9, 1940, Germany attacked Denmark and Norway in a typical blitzkrieg operation, the Swiss nation and army stood ready, in quite good shape to confront the onslaught that few doubted would come soon. It was expected to be a brutal surprise attack, without declaration of war, accompanied by the instruments of psychological warfare the Germans had used to some effect against the Scandinavian nations. To fend off these dangers, the government empowered the general to order, without further consultation, total mobilization in case of a surprise attack.

On April 18, 1940, the government and the commander-in-chief issued jointly an instruction to all members of the armed forces on how to act in case they were surprised by the outbreak of war while at home. Every officer and noncommissioned officer was instructed to gather all soldiers within his reach – when on leave or at home, they each carried a rifle and forty-eight rounds of ammunition – and to lead them against the enemy. In the absence of officers, every soldier had the duty to fight on his own initiative. The instruction contained a passage directed not only to the soldiers but to the whole nation, and it made a deep impression. It was admirable in its simple determination. The passage read: "If by radio, handbills or other media any information is transmitted casting doubt on the will of the Federal Council or of the Army High Command to resist an attacker, this information must be regarded as an invention of enemy propaganda."[9]

CHAPTER TWO

Secret Agreements for Survival

Military Necessity Versus Strict Neutrality

We have seen that the army high command and the general staff, like every thinking citizen, were convinced of the possibility, nay the probability, of a German attack. It was their professional duty to foresee every possible contingency. After the evaluation of all the different possible threats to the security of the country, they had to prepare, in the first place, for the most likely one, an attack from the northeast.

By May 10, 1940, the defense position facing north, as described, was ready. Its westernmost point, near the border toward France, was a fortress built into the solid rock of the Jura Mountains, which could cross the fire of its guns with the southernmost fort of the Maginot Line, on the Glaserberg across the national border. The location of the Swiss fort was dictated by facts of geography and elementary strategic thinking. It had been built as part of the framework of the general fortification program initiated in 1934. Yet the strategic situation as it evolved after March 1935, when Germany defied the Treaty of Versailles and openly began to rearm, made much wider thinking and planning necessary.

In the case of a German attack toward the west, against France as the traditional enemy and the ally and protector of the eastern European nations, it was certain that the Germans would try to outflank the French defenses in the north or in the south, or on both sides. A southern thrust would lead through Switzerland. For the Swiss planners such a threat had gradually become, in their thinking, a near probability. Therefore it seemed essential to them to insure against this contingency by providing for a certain degree of cooperation with the French army.

Even to think of cooperation planned in advance was, for a neutral country, a risky business. Any kind of contact, negotiation, or agreement could, if known to the Germans, be construed as a nonneutral act and even serve as a welcome pretext for a military attack. Such advanced planning, however, was not a new idea and was considered by the Swiss as absolutely conforming to the rights and duties of a neutral country. Contacts of this nature had existed in other critical periods of their history. Let us look back for a moment.[1]

As early as 1907 the chief of the Swiss general staff, Colonel Theophil von Sprecher, had exchanged papers called *Punktationen* with the German imperial general staff and had been received in Berlin by Moltke and by the Kaiser. There were also talks with the Austrian intelligence service. Those *Punktationen* stated the Swiss determination to remain neutral, to resist any aggression, and gave the conditions under which military assistance would be requested and accepted from the power opposing an aggressor.

Concerning the period of World War I, little is known of actual contacts with Germany or Austria over plans in the event of a French or an Italian violation of Swiss neutrality. It is reported that Ludendorff, the German *Generalquartiermeister*, when approached by a Swiss emissary, simply told him that no discussions or agreements were needed, since in such a situation Germany would take the necessary steps and issue the appropriate orders to the Swiss army. However, with the approaching defeat of Russia in 1917, which made the German armies in the east available for operations in the west, both the Allies and the Swiss feared that Ludendorff, in quest of an early termination of the war, might try to invade Switzerland. The attack could be directed across the Alps against Italy or across the Jura Mountains around the right flank of the French army. France therefore proposed an exchange of views about measures that such a contingency would dictate to both parties. In view of the violence and speed of all German operations of that time, early agreement on eventual cooperation in such an emergency seemed necessary. This was the view of the French high command, as communicated secretly to the Swiss counterpart. The Swiss government, when informed of the suggestion, agreed.

The then-Colonel Maxime Weygand, chief of staff of General Foch, was secretly received in Berne, in April 1917, by the chief of staff of the Swiss army, Corps Commander von Sprecher. An unwritten understanding was reached, stating where the Swiss would set up their main line of resistance and defining the axes by which French forces would advance in the rear to buttress that position. The necessary engineering work for improving roads and railroads for the French troop movements was agreed upon and thereupon executed by the Swiss.[2]

Years before World War II, the head of the federal military department, Minister of Defense Rudolf Minger, discussed the problem of new contacts with Henri Guisan, who at that time commanded the First Army Corps and was a trusted friend. It was decided that, without informing any other member of the government, Guisan should use his good personal relations with high officers of the French army to initiate a confidential exchange of views.

Minger, a real farmer running his own farm not far from the federal capital, had been a member of Parliament, was elected to the government in 1929, and had assumed, in 1931, the direction of military affairs. Soon he became a popular figure. I can still see him when he inspected troops: on horseback, in civilian clothes — yellow riding breeches, black cutaway, and black bowler hat — drawing enthusiastic applause from the civilian onlookers. His popularity was due to his peasant origin, his simple ways, and his courage in fighting for a more modern army. Hundreds of wry anecdotes concerning his simplicity went the rounds. Under these appearances he was a shrewd politician who succeeded in winning wide support for a program to modernize the army, not an easy task in the atmosphere prevailing in the early thirties. During this time, Henri Guisan became his trusted adviser. When in 1939 a supreme commander had to be elected, there was, luckily for the country and due to Minger's careful political groundwork, no hesitation about the choice to make.

Contacts with France

Guisan took things in hand, but, being a clever and prudent peasant, did not engage himself personally. He entrusted the first contacts to a personal friend, Lieutenant Colonel Albert de Tscharner, who had served in the French Foreign Legion, was a World War I hero, and now lived in retirement on the shores of Lake Geneva. He also instructed an officer of his staff, Major Samuel Gonard, who had been a brilliant student at the *Ecole de guerre* in Paris, to establish contacts with generals Gamelin and Georges. As a juridical consultant on questions of international law and neutrality he took into his confidence Claude du Pasquier, professor at the University of Neuchâtel and also a colonel on the general staff.[3]

Talks began in Paris and at different places in Switzerland. During official visits to maneuvers in France and Italy, Guisan met Gamelin and Georges, and during maneuvers in Switzerland, Marshal Pétain. In October 1938, Guisan was invited by General de Lattre de Tassigny to a secret inspection tour of the Maginot Line between the Swiss border and Strasbourg. The minister of defense expressly authorized the visit. Dressed as a tourist, unaccompanied, and in absolute secret, Guisan left Berne on a late train for Strasbourg. By chance the military attaché of the Netherlands in Berne boarded the same train and, delighted to find good company, asked Guisan whether he could join him. It was a comical and delicate situation. Guisan could not tell the Dutchman where he was going and why, and he could only hope that de Lattre de Tassigny would not roll out the red carpet at Strasbourg. He was greatly relieved to find the general alone at the station. The Dutch officer evidently guessed what was on and was intelligent enough to keep the secret.

Shortly before the outbreak of the war, Guisan's chief of

staff, Colonel Edouard Petitpierre, met generals Gamelin and Georges in Paris, and they examined the project of a military convention but without trying to reach an agreement.

When the Swiss army was mobilized on September 2, 1939, Bernard Barbey, a successful Swiss novelist living in Paris who was also a cavalry officer and a major on the general staff, duly returned home, put on his uniform, and reported for service. Because of his interesting and wide connections in France, he was at once enlisted in the intelligence service under Colonel Roger Masson.

While he was living in Paris, Barbey had met an engineer, who also was a journalist and writer, called André Garteiser. Garteiser had contributed articles to the *Revue hebdomadaire*, of which Barbey was the editor. Impressed by the intelligence, experience, and personality of Garteiser, Barbey had introduced him to the chief of staff of the Swiss First Army Corps who, in turn, presented him to his commander, Guisan. Chance had it that Garteiser was at Guisan's home, *Verte Rive*, near Lausanne, on August 30, 1939, the day of the election of the general. At the outbreak of the war, Garteiser, a French reserve officer, joined the staff of General Georges and was entrusted with the liaison between the French high command and the French Eighth Army located near the Swiss border. This connection paved the way for a continued liaison with the French high command, a liaison not likely to arouse suspicion. Barbey could travel to Paris and back under the pretext of work for the publishing firm of Fayard, of which he was the *directeur littéraire*, and for the periodical of which he was the editor.

On September 24, 1939, Barbey was ordered to see the general, who informed him of the earlier discussions with the French. He was instructed to go to Paris and find out how the Garteiser connection could be used for reaching an informal but a tangible understanding on eventual emergency measures. Detailed instructions were given by Lieutenant Colonel Gonard, who now had become chief of the general's personal staff.[4]

Barbey visited Paris and the front line north of Basel together with Garteiser, and Garteiser came to Switzerland

and was shown the terrain over which a defensive battle might be fought. On December 2, 1939, Major Barbey was received in the castle of Vincennes by the French generalissimo, Gamelin; on the sixth he saw at La Ferté the commander-in-chief of the eastern front, General Georges, and at Dole the commander of the Eighth Army, General Besson. The latter explained his plan to occupy, upon Swiss request, the heights south of Basel, the plateau of Gempen, where the two armies would join hands. Besson felt that the initial maneuver would not require more than four hours. All the French generals explicitly accepted the Swiss *conditio sine qua non* for any cooperation, namely, that they would never penetrate Swiss territory unless requested to do so by the Swiss high command.

The heights of Gempen south of Basel became the center of interest since it was there that the lineup between the two armies would be made. On his frequent visits to Switzerland and upon Gonard's request, Lieutenant Colonel Garteiser even brought plans for the construction of shelters for the French artillery to be installed on the heights of Gempen. Building of these shelters actually started.

In order to create some symmetry essential for a neutral's duties and to keep up appearances in case the Germans got wind of the contacts with France, a mission similar to Barbey's was dispatched to the German high command. It was entrusted to Major Hans Berli, who, as a captain, had attended staff courses in Germany from 1933 to 1935 and was well acquainted with the leading men of the *Wehrmacht.* His mission was so successfully kept secret that no report or any document revealing its results has been found. Berli died suddenly during a military exercise in 1952, when he was a division commander, and he took his secret with him to the grave.[5]

In March 1940, Barbey again saw generals Gamelin and Georges. The two repeated how much they regretted that they never could establish contacts with the Belgian high command similar to those now existing with the Swiss. They feared that this omission – due to the reluctance and hostility of the Belgians – might, perhaps very soon, seriously jeopardize the defensive movements against a German operation in the north.

In April, an official Swiss military mission was invited to visit the Maginot Line. Its head, Colonel Montfort, knew absolutely nothing of the secret dealings with France. On the other hand, Lieutenant Colonel Gonard, who stood at the center of the negotiations, participated in the tour as a silent observer. The two returned with a very gloomy view on the spirit and state of preparation of the French forces.

Six weeks later, on June 9 when the French armies were already reeling under their terrible defeat, Barbey was received at Vincennes near Paris by the new commander-in-chief, General Weygand. The general remembered his mission to Switzerland in 1917 and sadly remarked that the support the Swiss could expect, in case of being attacked, might be on the order of only one division, instead of a whole army group as planned.[6]

The Swiss were treading on thin ice. A misunderstanding could easily have provoked action by officers who by now had standing orders for establishing the liaison with well-defined French forces. An example: During the night of May 14/15 an air force officer, Colonel Borel, instructed to join the French air staff near the Swiss border, was awakened at his quarters in Zofingen by a telephone call. He immediately made ready to join the assigned post in France. On the point of leaving in his automobile, he was stopped – it turned out that the wrong number had been called. The same night – the night on which, according to all available intelligence reports, the Germans were to attack – a French battalion emerged out of the dark at the Swiss border, at the point where the Maginot Line ended. The commander announced to the Swiss officer in charge of the barricade closing the road that the Germans had irrupted into Basel, that Switzerland was at war with Germany, and that as an advance party for much more important forces he had to occupy a sector on Swiss territory assigned to him. The captain at the frontier calmly explained to his early visitor that the information was untrue, that no German attack had been reported, and that no French intervention had been requested. Therefore he could not let him enter with his men. After some hesitation the French turned around and disappeared in the early morning mist.[7]

No doubt a wrong movement on either side might have had far-reaching consequences. The French 240-mm guns trained on the bridges of Basel might have opened fire, the Germans might have tried to cross the Rhine, and Switzerland would have been in the war – on which side?

Documents in German Hands

On June 17, 1940, France sued for an armistice, which was signed at Rethondes on June 22. The outstanding problem for the Swiss was to keep the secret of the negotiations and agreements as completely as possible. General Guisan ordered the documents concerning France, which had been tucked away in a safe in a medieval castle somewhere in Switzerland, brought back to headquarters where he had them destroyed. He did not know that on June 16 the Germans had already found, in La Charité-sur-Loire, an abandoned railway van full of documents evacuated from Paris and that among them were papers and maps concerning the negotiations with Switzerland.[8]

It was almost a miracle that the secret had been kept, or almost kept, for so long. Barbey had been in Paris eleven times, Garteiser in Switzerland ten times and at the border six times. A dozen Swiss officers had been instructed to establish contact with certain French formations immediately after a German attack. The French Eighth Army had issued standing orders concerning eventual aid to the Swiss.[9] But was the secret really kept? In France, too many people knew about the orders concerning an eventual move into Switzerland. And after incidents like those of May 15 it was highly improbable that the German intelligence, which had its ears everywhere, was not aware of at least part of the truth.

Just how wise it had been of Guisan not to inform the government (except Federal Councillor Minger, who had suggested the whole operation) was demonstrated as early as March 1940 when the German minister in Berne, Otto Carl Köcher, had got wind of cetain secret dealings and directly mentioned these "rumors" to the Swiss foreign minister and then president, Pilet-Golaz. Pilet-Golaz, in good faith, could completely deny such allegations.

The papers seized by the German army at the railway station of La Charité-sur-Loire were transmitted to the German high command. It seems that as early as July 29, 1940, the military sent a list and synopsis of the documents to Hitler. Then they transferred all the material to a special study group set up in Berlin under Ambassador Hans Adolf von Moltke, which had the task of exploiting the sensational find. It contained, of course, much more material than the thin folder concerning Switzerland. In November a report on the secret agreements between Guisan and Gamelin was sent to the German foreign minister, Joachim von Ribbentrop, who drew Hitler's attention to it.

The Swiss government was warned of the dangerous discovery through different channels, among them probably the head of the German intelligence service, Admiral Wilhelm Canaris, and members of the foreign service. As early as October 16, 1940, the Swiss legation in Berlin learned that the documents were being translated from the original French into German. It seemed now almost certain that Hitler planned to use them against Switzerland, by casting doubt on the sincerity of its neutrality and accusing it of dealings with Germany's enemies. The information was also "leaked" in Berlin to Swiss visitors—among them Colonel Gustav Däniker—who were known to be pro-German and likely to use it, upon their return, against General Guisan and those around him.

It is certain that the SS and Ribbentrop considered the documents of La Charité to be a powerful weapon by which they might even move Hitler to order the "liquidation" of Switzerland, which they warmly advocated. Since a favorable moment for the execution of their wish had to be awaited, instructions were issued to deny the existence of the documents, to refrain from mentioning them, and to hold them back as a secret weapon. They were to be kept for a later moment, when they would be used. Their sudden and brutal publication then would, it was thought, provoke the fall of General Guisan, throw the Swiss people off balance, and make the Swiss, caught in such a situation of shock by a surprise attack, fall easy prey to the National Socialists.

General Guisan, requested by the government to give it the facts about the dealings with France, simply stated that *he* had not entered into any binding agreement, which was literally true. He added that as early as 1939 he had commissioned the general staff to make parallel studies concerning eventual cooperation with one of the belligerents in case the other attacked the country, as had been done in World War I.

In his own mind, however, throughout the war years Guisan pondered the question of how and when the documents of La Charité-sur-Loire might be used against Switzerland. He wondered whether the planned cooperation with France in the case of a German attack would not be interpreted in Berlin in a way that would encourage a German preventive or preemptive strike at the moment they thought a strike by the Allies was being planned. In late 1942 and early 1943, after the Allied landing in northern Africa, the danger of Allied operations through Italy and Switzerland became, as the Swiss military intelligence learned, a serious preoccupation for the German supreme command. It was evident that, knowing the overwhelming sympathy the Allied cause enjoyed in Switzerland and with the background of the documents on cooperation with France, the Germans doubted whether Guisan would resist a thrust by the Allies. General Guisan, therefore, as we shall see, did everything to dispel the German doubts. He authorized quite unusual contacts between the Swiss and the German intelligence services in the hope of achieving this. The order of operations W42 of September 1, 1942, which contemplated simultaneous resistance against an Allied and a German invasion, was definitely linked with the traumatic experience of La Charité.

CHAPTER THREE

The Hurricane Breaks Loose

The Attack Is for Tonight

On May 10, 1940, at an early hour, I walked over to the antiaircraft battery of which, at that time, I was the commanding officer. The battery was positioned near the little town of Olten where the two main railroad lines running up from Italy meet. Orders had been received some days previously to be always on full alert at daybreak. The officer in charge met me at the entrance to the gun site and informed me that the Netherlands and Belgium had been invaded by the Germans and that a German attack had been launched on the western front. High up and far to the north, well out of the range of our 75-mm Vickers guns, we could distinguish airplanes, brilliant little spots moving in the blue sky.

While we watched the air space over the important strategic railroad center that we were ordered to defend against bombers and parachute troops, and while in other sectors ten thousand eyes looked across the Rhine or from mountain peaks and passes into the neighboring land where German forces were supposed to be massing in preparation for an attack, full mobilization of the Swiss army had again begun. Within twenty-four hours, 450,000 men were under arms, now well trained and most of them in prepared, fortified positions. From the western borders of the country additional regiments were moved into specific sectors of the Army Position.

On the previous day the military police had learned that a raid by saboteurs was planned against General Guisan's headquarters. He quietly drove to a nearby château, where the chief of the general staff awaited him and where they spent the night, well protected by strong infantry forces and connected with their respective staffs by radio and hastily laid telephone cables. The military police who waited around the general's headquarters for the saboteurs waited in vain.

When, toward May 14, the German advance in northern France seemed to lose momentum, the Allied high command at Vincennes became convinced that the next move would be a massive attack on Switzerland, with the purpose of initiating another turning movement around the southern wing of the Maginot Line. The Swiss government and the general staff were informed from Paris of this imminent danger. In Rome, the Swiss military attaché was confidentially warned by an Italian "friend" in a high place. Military intelligence reports mentioned massive concentrations—thirty German divisions—north of the Rhine where it forms the frontier between Germany and Switzerland. Material for building bridges was visibly displayed on the northern banks of the river.[1]

The Swiss army was now in utmost readiness. The orders were to expect a German assault in the early hours of the fifteenth. General Guisan, after having heard with his staff a full report by the head of the intelligence service, ending with the assertion that the attack was planned for the following morning, retired to his rooms completely unmoved with the remark, "See you tomorrow. Good night."

As far as I could see when observing the officers and soldiers under my command, beneath their calm exterior there was an excited expectation, coupled with a kind of incredulity. This was easy to understand in an army that had trained and trained, yet had never seen a war. Some of the men seemed to look forward to a real fight, some seemed to think that such a thing simply could not happen to us, but nobody looked scared.

We now know that no attack was planned, but that false information had been planted everywhere in order to make sure that the French armies in the south would not be moved north where they were badly needed for the reinforcing of the tottering front. With hindsight it is clear that the German preparations opposite the Swiss border were much too obvious to be true.

May 15 passed. The unforeseen turn of events in France soon created an altogether different situation. The Swiss army had to adapt to it and did, fast and efficiently. What happened to the civilian population in those critical days is a different story.

The Defeat of France

The events, as they developed after the middle of May, came as a nightmare to the Swiss. Few well-informed men in the army high command or in the intelligence service had realized the sorry state of the French army—its morale, its training, and its equipment—or that its high command was inept. In the main, people had before their eyes the victorious army of 1918 and the impregnable Maginot Line. They followed anxiously the war reports on the radio and in the newspapers, and particularly the course of the battle in the west. When it was announced on May 17 that German Army Group A had reached the river Oise, all who knew what that signified lost hope.[2] I shall never forget the moment when the French communiqué was read on the 12:30 news, ending with the ominous words; "We have now entered upon the phase of a war of movement." We looked at each other and one of us said, "This means *sauve qui peut* [every man for himself]."

On June 16 Guderian's panzers, as expected, reached the Swiss border near the French town of Pontarlier and turned northeast, taking the Maginot Line from the rear. The French Forty-fifth Army Corps—consisting of one French division, one Polish division, and one brigade of Spahis—was driven from the west toward the borders of Switzerland. On June 19 its commander asked to be allowed to cross into Switzerland to be interned.[3] Forty-two thousand men now streamed across the border over two narrow roads, dropped their

weapons at the feet of the Swiss soldiers without slowing
down their pace, and then marched on toward the interior.
The situation was not easy to handle, since at the same time
equipment and reserves for the Swiss army were moving in
the opposite direction. A new Swiss defensive system had by
now been organized on a front toward the northwest, confronting the massed German forces gathering in conquered
France. Had Guderian's panzers struck at the same moment,
chaos and tragedy could hardly have been avoided. However, the Germans had other objectives in mind, and if they
ever intended to attack Switzerland, they felt sure that they
could do it later at a better moment.

Right from May 10 and throughout the battle of France and
the rapidly developing catastrophe of the French armies, a
year of psychological warfare and subversion bore fruit. In
Belgium and the Netherlands, and before them in Norway,
according to reports everybody could read and hear, saboteurs and parachute forces had attacked everywhere. Spies
and agents were now believed to be omnipresent. The mass
flight of the Belgian and French populace had begun, and it
spread panic far and wide. Swiss officers and soldiers, to
whom it would never have occurred to abandon their posts in
front of the enemy and who certainly were no cowards, now
telephoned their families urging them to leave their homes
and run for shelter in the western part of the country or in the
high mountains. Psychologically it must have been a mixture
of simple panic and a desire to appear important and well-
informed in the eyes of their loved ones. There was also the
inability to realize that this was not just another of the many
military exercises with live ammunition where you could tell
people to get out of the danger zone and the target area.

When, in the fall of 1939, the builders of the Army Position
had begun their work and everybody could see with his own
eyes what areas of Switzerland would inevitably fall into
enemy hands and where the main fighting and consequent
destruction would be, some people began to take protective
measures. Business firms, well-heeled families, and those responsible for cultural treasures began to prepare shelters in
areas which were – naively – thought to be safe. Corporations

moved their archives, some even their head offices, to the west of the country. The shores of Lake Leman (Lake Geneva) held, in this process, a special attraction. Families rented chalets in a pretty mountain setting, where women and children could go in case of danger. The more important items of the museums were stored underground. Medieval stained-glass windows were removed from churches and town halls, packed, and sent to places of safety.

Local governments, unsure of what to do with the population in the zone of the prospective front line, asked the federal authorities for guidance, without receiving, however, any clear answer. Therefore, the municipalities hinted vaguely that a time might come when it would be better for the population to move to the interior of the country. Yet nothing actually was planned or ordered – the reality of war simply was beyond these good men's powers of imagination.

Thus the psychologically unprepared or ill-prepared masses were suddenly confronted with the events of May. Many people thought that probably the moment had now come when they were expected to evacuate the danger zone. An unseemly stream of refugees began to move westward across the country. Many of them were rich people with a car and a place to go. The overwhelming majority of the people, of course, and not only the poorer classes as some historians and pseudohistorians try to make out, remained fatalistically where they happened to be. Some of the schools in Zurich, among them the Gymnasium, where at that time the sons of the elite studied, were closed on May 11 for a week but for an altogether different reason. Fifty percent of the teachers had joined the army, some of the rest were on duty as anti-air-raid wardens, some of the older students were mobilized for the air force as auxiliaries on observation posts. Organized teaching had become impossible. So the rest of the students were sent to help on the farms, where the men also had been mobilized. It is, as we see, unlikely that very many families fled.

Nobody knows what would have occurred had war really broken out – perhaps a panic similar to the one that was sweeping France. The spectacle offered by a relatively small portion of the population was unpleasant enough. On that critical night I was standing with a few soldiers in front of my command post, after being alerted. The building, an old school, stood where an important yet secondary east-west road passes. A long, almost unbroken line of automobiles rolled past, the cars heavily packed with women and children, some even with a mattress slung over the top, which the occupants fondly hoped would protect against strafing. The soldiers looked on at the spectacle, half amused, half incredulous. It seemed far away from us, none of our concern; we had no feeling for these people, who seemed strangers, not belonging to our world.

The evacuation and flight of part of the population was not as shameful really as it appears to many a present-day observer. It may be compared with the attitude of the British people, who later, under attack, proved so heroic. In the early phases of the war, the British, as unprepared as the Swiss for confronting the realities of a modern war, behaved not less unrealistically.

It was only when the devastation of Rotterdam and the extent of the destruction of other cities became fully known that the local governments of Swiss cities and cantons began to look seriously at the problem. Until now nobody had questioned the wisdom or the feasibility of the defense of a city, say of the size of Zurich. Everybody seemed to accept the idea of total destruction of an urban center of this size and importance. Yet what actually happened was not that the citizens and the city fathers were filled with heroic self-abnegation, but that they lacked imagination and were uninformed. Nobody had actually taken the possibility seriously — it was simply beyond the imagination of people brought up in peace and order. As late as June 3, 1940, the government of the canton of Zurich posted a letter addressed to the federal government — they did not bother to send a telegram or a delegation to Berne. In the letter they declared that they firmly stood behind the decision to defend Zurich. But had the Federal Council or the military command ever thought of the fate of 350,000 inhabitants for whom there was no protection whatsoever? Defense of the city without previous evacuation of the people now seemed unthinkable to them.[4]

Such questions had to be answered and the civilian authorities did not know what to say. So the military authorities had to reply. They did reply, brutally, but there was no other way out. On June 20, 1940, General Guisan issued, over his own signature, an instruction to the populace to the effect that everybody, under all circumstances, had to stay at home unless otherwise instructed by explicit military order.

The crisis passed, fortunately without the catastrophic consequences the total unpreparedness would have had for hundreds of thousands of people. Gradually those who had fled returned quietly. It is estimated, however, that 2,000 inhabitants of Basel, who were ashamed or too frightened, remained where they had fled – at Lake Geneva, in an alpine village, or in the United States.

Battle in the Air

The development of air forces and the consequent prospect of war in the air were bound to create new problems for the neutral countries. Most facets of the rights and duties of a neutral were well defined in international law. It was generally admitted that any attempt by a belligerent to penetrate a neutral's territory – irrespective of whether the neutral state was the target of an aggression or whether a belligerent only wanted to cross neutral territory in the course of his operations against an opponent – was to be considered as a military attack to be resisted and repelled by the neutral. In such a situation, neutrality automatically came to an end – as the cases of Denmark, Norway, the Netherlands, and Belgium demonstrated.

Armed penetration of the airspace of neutral countries was tacitly considered a different matter. Whereas the neutral has the unquestioned right and duty to repel such penetrations, the act of crossing the airspace and the act of repelling the transgressor by force were not considered to be acts of war terminating neutrality and drawing the neutral into the war.

Thus, the Swiss did not hesitate to engage their fighters and antiaircraft artillery to stop aerial incursions, and the Germans did not hesitate to fight back. Yet the incidents arising from this did not alter the fact that the countries concerned remained legally at peace. Had the Germans, in this contest, committed an aggression that involved fighting on the ground—a close possibility at one time, as we shall see—it would have been a quite different matter. It would have meant all-out war between the Axis and Switzerland.

What we saw in those early hours of May 10 were German and French airplanes, battling over French soil and often inadvertently crossing the Swiss border. From then until the end of May 1940, a total of 113 foreign airplanes penetrated the neutral airspace; in June the number was 84. In the very first days two German bombers, surprised in Swiss airspace by Swiss air patrols, were fired on and hit. One, heavily damaged, made a forced landing, the other escaped across the border, burning and leaving a smoke trail. On June 1 a German bomber was shot down by a Swiss fighter pilot near Neuchâtel, another, fired on near the border, crashed on French soil. The following day another bomber was forced to land, damaged, in Switzerland. From now on when they planned to cross Swiss airspace, the German bombers were escorted by Me-110 fighters, with orders to engage the Swiss Me-109s. Three Swiss planes, one of them a slow observation plane, were shot down over Switzerland by the Germans. In these engagements, Swiss fighter pilots in their turn shot down four German planes. Bombs fell, mostly at night, in the border areas.[5]

In these fights the Swiss pilots had shown considerable dash and skill. The Germans were outraged, especially because the Swiss were using airplanes bought from Germany. In diplomatic notes Berlin accused the Swiss of penetrating into the French airspace in pursuit of German planes. In retaliation Goering dispatched a sabotage group with orders to blow up Swiss air bases; as we shall later see, the group was arrested on June 16 before it achieved anything.

The defense of neutral airspace against penetration by the air forces engaged in the war posed many difficult problems. Neither the Swiss fighter command nor the antiaircraft artillery was equipped to operate at night. The few German-constructed searchlights with acoustic detection gear, bought shortly before the war, were ineffective. When the Royal Air Force began its bomber raids against Italy and southern Germany in the summer of 1940, it did not, of course, respect Swiss airspace. The Swiss antiaircraft batteries with their searchlights were moved tentatively to strategic points under the air lanes where the British bombers were most likely to pass and, if possible, were set up on high mountain sites in order to increase range. Some batteries were positioned near Berne, where nightly the Axis diplomats could hear, along with the drone of the bombers' engines, the antiaircraft artillery fire and see the shells exploding against the night sky. It was quite a spectacle, yet without radar and many more searchlights it was impossible to score a hit. As was to be expected, the Germans, in indignant terms, accused the Swiss air force of not trying to oppose these incursions. There were many wry anecdotes on this theme going the rounds at the time. The truth, however, was that the existing equipment and armament simply did not make for any success in darkness. To one of the German protests, the federal government answered with a question, Why was it that the Germans themselves did not stop the British bombers when they flew hundreds of kilometers over German territory or over territory occupied by the German armies?[6]

One thing angered the Germans and Italians still more than the failure of the Swiss air force to take effective action against the British bombers. Switzerland, with all its brightly lit cities and villages, was a powerful beacon in the middle of a continent that otherwise was under total blackout. So Berlin began to demand that Switzerland should introduce the blackout on the German model. Fully aware that this would be interpreted by the Allies as a cowardly concession to Germany, the Federal Council opposed the demand. It used all kinds of arguments, among them that a blackout would endanger the safety of the railroads in which the Axis powers were so much interested. Also the general was against such a measure, since he quite rightly thought that it would increase the danger of bombs being dropped by mistake on Switzerland.

After a few particularly heavy British raids across Swiss airspace in October and November 1940, the general, who had already been empowered in September by the civilian authority to do so, yielded to the pressures he knew the Axis exercised on the government and ordered a total blackout on November 6, 1940. It lasted until September 12, 1944, when the battles along the Swiss borders made aerial incursions even more frequent than before. The blackout, more than being an inconvenience, had a deep moral effect. It showed how much Switzerland had become a prisoner in Axis-dominated Europe.

Exactly as predicted by the air force, the blackout increased the danger of accidental bombings. In December 1940 bombs fell on Basel and Zurich; in October 1941, on a village in the border area; in May 1943, on Zurich and the fluvial port of Basel. In February 1941, the British foreign minister, Anthony Eden, transmitted the apologies for certain bombings of His Majesty's Government in eloquent terms, which were, at the same time, an impressive reminder to the neutral country of what it owed to the British. Eden said among other things:

> fighting as they are for the traditions of freedom and resistance to tyranny, of which the Swiss Confederation has in former times been the protagonist in European history, His Majesty's Government feel entitled to count on the collaboration of the Swiss authorities while a full investigation is being made . . . , and to claim the forbearance of the Swiss people in judging two tragic accidents.[7]

Early in 1943 the British asked for the abolition of the blackout, arguing that this would protect Switzerland from accidental bombing.

On January 27, 1943, the American air force began its daylight raids on Germany, Italy, and the occupied countries. Aerial incursions became more and more frequent. The gravest incident occurred on April 1, 1944, when twenty U.S. bombers dropped four hundred bombs on the city of Schaffhausen by mistake. The error of the group's commander can easily be explained by the location of the city. It is situated on the northern bank of the Rhine, and while over wide stretches the river forms the border between Germany and Switzerland, at this particular place Swiss territory extends north of the river. There were one hundred fifty casualties and half a hundred buildings destroyed. In February 1945 two other small cities, Rafz and Stein, north of the Rhine were accidentally bombed and strafed, with forty-four casualties.[8]

The blunders were immediately admitted and compensation was promised, including reparations for valuable works of art that had been destroyed. An amount of $62 million was paid by Washington in 1949. Some unpleasant haggling, for which the Swiss were responsible with their ludicrous insistence on payment of interest from the day of the bombing, preceded the settlement. The question of interest gave rise to a heated debate in the U.S. Congress, which reflected significant American views about Switzerland's neutrality. One congressman from Ohio thought the Swiss were "impertinent," that they had enriched themselves during two world wars, and that Switzerland had been, in between, the meeting place of Fascist warmongers. Another congressman, from Missouri, said that Switzerland's neutrality had been a "phony neutrality" because the American aircrews had been interned instead of being sent back to continue the fight, etc.[9]

Although regretting the loss of life caused by these incidents, the Swiss people on the whole, in contrast to their government, showed great understanding for the mistakes made by the Allied air forces and were fully aware of the fact that they were also fighting for Switzerland. The number of aerial incursions increased as the Allied landing in France approached and the war drew ever closer. To give examples: in February 1944 there were 500 incidents; in April, 650.

One summer morning, a pilotless Flying Fortress – the crew having parachuted from their crippled aircraft – glided, gradually losing height, over northern Switzerland. It collided with the tower of a medieval castle, which happened to be the summer residence of Professor Max Huber, then the president of the International Committee of the Red Cross. The plane caught fire and flaming gasoline and exploding ammunition poured down into the interior of the tower, where the professor's priceless library on international peace was installed. Only the preceding day a Zurich machine factory had brought its archives, for safety from accidental bombing, to the same tower. The children playing in the castle courtyard ducked for safety, and courageous men rescued some of the archives from the burning wreckage. Nobody was hurt, but the library was totally lost. Huber, at Red Cross headquarters in Geneva, was informed over the telephone of the accident. He answered, "Don't worry. It is nothing compared with what I see every day."

General Carl Spaatz, commander of the U.S. Air Force in Europe, visited Berne on March 3, 1945, and measures were agreed upon for reducing violations of neutral airspace. Most of the violations, of course, were far from being intentional and were often caused by aircraft in distress. The Swiss air force and the antiaircraft artillery therefore received orders to warn aircraft penetrating the Swiss airspace by radio, rocket signals, or artillery salvos across the bows. The Swiss were permitted to shoot in earnest only if the warnings were not heeded.

In the course of the whole war, a total of 250 belligerent airplanes landed or crashed in Switzerland, of which 15 were shot down by the Swiss air force and 9 by antiaircraft artillery. A total of 40 Liberators and Flying Fortresses alone landed at Dübendorf, the military air base near Zurich. There were days when as many as a dozen of them landed—having run out of fuel, with wounded men on board, or otherwise in trouble.

A most interesting case presented itself on April 28, 1944, when a German Me-110 in distress was guided by the Swiss radio control to land at Dübendorf. On inspection it was discovered that it carried the most modern and secret radar equipment the Germans had developed. Berlin requested the immediate return of the plane. The Swiss refused. Berlin then planned to destroy the plane on the ground with bombs or by a strike by parachute troops. The secret equipment, however, had been taken immediately to a hidden underground shelter in the Alps. The destruction of the plane, as planned by Goering's men, would have meant war with Switzerland

and, since the secret equipment had already been removed anyway, would have been completely useless. So a compromise was reached and war was averted. The Swiss air force agreed to bring the ultrasecret equipment back to the plane and to burn it on the ground together with the airplane, in the presence of the German air attaché and other witnesses. The Germans, in turn, had to agree to another side of the deal: They had to deliver twelve of the newest Me-109 G fighters, complete with arms and ammunition, which the Swiss badly needed as replacements for lost aircraft.[10]

There were also odd, amusing incidents. One afternoon in November 1944 I was watching an American Flying Fortress approaching the Magadino air base in the south of Switzerland, prior to landing. The plane was escorted down by two Swiss fighter planes, which looked like tiny mosquitoes, each with its distinctive white cross in a red field shining in the evening sun. They evidently had signaled to the American pilot that he was in neutral airspace and had forced him to land. On the following day the commanding officer of the air base told me that he had asked the American commander of the plane, which was in perfect fighting condition, why he had not opened fire on the Swiss fighters and had not tried to escape. The answer was, "Why, it would never occur to me to shoot at a Red Cross plane!"

This narrative of the battle in the air has anticipated events, jumping from the most dangerous period of the war to the concluding, more relaxed times. In between, however, prolonged periods of crisis and anxiety had to be overcome.

Encircled – Discouraged

The capitulation of France on June 17, 1940, came as a deep shock to the Swiss. They had firmly believed – because they wanted to believe – in the military power of France. Now defeatism spread like wildfire among the neutral observers. In the French-speaking part of Switzerland, so close in its thinking and feeling to France, the defeat of the invincible French army produced profound distress. If the war was now over for the French, many people thought that it was also over for the Swiss. Discouragement spread. To many, the immediate demobilization of the Swiss army seemed the order of the day. As far as the German-speaking majority of the country was concerned, for whom the hatred of National Socialist Germany was deep-rooted, opinions were divided. Some – probably the majority – were desperately resolved to resist at any cost if the Germans now turned on Switzerland. Others – certainly in the minority, but vocal – advocated a course directed at appeasing the Germans, buying peace and continued independence by making political concessions to the triumphant Axis powers. Their power, so impressively illustrated by the victory over France, seemed enhanced by the fact that at that time the Soviet Union was the ally of Hitler's Germany. The Soviets had conquered Finland in the winter war of 1939/40, and their colossal weight, added to Germany's power, led many an observer to believe that the threat hanging over the still-free nations was irresistible. Also the slogan, spread from Berlin, that a New Europe was now emerging appealed, of course, to people of all classes eager to adopt the latest fashion. A minority in the Swiss government, among them President Pilet-Golaz and Federal Councillor Ernst Wetter, the minister of finance, were of a similar opinion. They may not have believed in earnest in a New Europe, but they thought that the Axis powers were going to dominate western Europe for a long time and that it was their duty to arrange matters with the Germans as best they could. They advocated a partial demobilization of the army – the foreign minister in the hope of pleasing the Germans, the finance minister yielding to pressures from industry and the trade unions. By July 7, 1940, the Swiss forces under arms were reduced by two-thirds.

The government decided, too late, that it now had to give some guidance to a bewildered people. After a lengthy discussion between three members of the government and a member of Parliament entrusted with press relations between the army and the government, the president of the confederation, Marcel Pilet-Golaz, addressed the nation over the radio. He spoke in French on June 25, 1940. Only two members of the government, who had to read the president's speech at the microphone in German and Italian translations respectively, saw the manuscript of the speech beforehand, and then only minutes before delivery. Pilet's speech sounded as if Switzerland had been defeated; it appealed to the people to rally unquestioningly behind the government, which would act with authority. The authoritarian trend, visibly copied from Marshal Pétain's style, and the affirmation that the free and easy way of life had come to an end sounded ominous. The Swiss army was only mentioned in one sentence announcing that it would gradually be demobilized. Not a word of thanks to the soldiers; not a word about resisting an eventual aggressor. It was a speech that could have perfectly well reflected the mood of a defeated and disorganized nation.[11]

President Pilet-Golaz has remained a controversial figure ever since. His case is of interest beyond the narrow Swiss scene, since he belongs to that group of statesmen whose fate it was to try to coexist with the National Socialist and Fascist systems of violence and lawlessness. This group of statesmen of one of the most dramatic periods of modern history also included Neville Chamberlain, Marshal Stalin, Marshal Pétain, Pope Pius XII, King Leopold III of the Belgians, Joseph Beck, and Edward Benes. A comprehensive psychological history of them still has to be written. Marcel Pilet-Golaz was an intellectual of great intelligence, and he was sure that he could do better than anybody else. His sin was vanity, and it was his belief that none but he could fulfill the special mission of keeping Switzerland out of the war.[12] His personality was closely linked with the spiritual landscape in which he grew up, namely, the city of Lausanne. Lausanne is the small capital of the canton of Vaud, a canton that at Pilet-Golaz's time was still thoroughly agricultural in character. The city had, in sharp contrast with its canton, a lively intellectual life oriented toward and inspired from Paris. Igor Stravinsky, Ernest Ansermet, and Charles-Ferdinand Ramuz are names connected with it. The Lausanne intellectual draws, from the spiritual distance that separates him from his closest neighbors, a feeling of superiority, which prevents him from seeing that he is, in a wider sense, a provincial. Pilet-Golaz was one of these intellectuals. I had two meetings with him, and I found that he was convinced he knew everything and had no interest in listening to what somebody else had to say. For these reasons he had no contact with his fellow Vaudois General Guisan, who was, for him, "a peasant."[13]

Reactions to the president's speech of June 25 were slow coming in. Most people and indeed most members of the government and of parliament had difficulty at first in interpreting Pilet's elegant and obscure verbiage. The people were bewildered, the Allies were surprised, and the Germans, who interpreted the speech as a declaration of submission to the authoritarian Europe they were proposing to build, were overjoyed. To many it seemed likely that the Federal Council was planning to take an authoritarian course – nobody knew at the time that the speech had been written and delivered without its contents having been discussed and approved by the government. The Germans and the pro-German organizations in Switzerland applauded. After a few days of hesitation, critical voices swelled into an impressive chorus – as impressive as it could be considering the tight regulations the press had to work under at that time. Actually, on the surface, nothing happened. Nothing was changed; government and army continued to function as usual. Many units were sent home; the rest guarded the frontiers and went on with their training.

The high command was deeply concerned, but not discouraged. It knew that now what was most needed was to show a bold face to the Germans. After the armistice with France, Colonel Iwan von Ilsemann, the German military attaché, visited the Swiss chief of staff, Jakob Huber, at headquarters. He gave a glowing account of the German feats of arms in the battle of France, and the chief of staff listened in silence, chewing as always his cheap cigar (*Stumpen*). When von Ilsemann had finished, he looked eagerly at Huber's face where he thought he was sure to read the deep impression his tale had made. Huber sat silent for a moment, then, slowly putting the cigar on the table, said, "Here – nobody will pass."

Huber had been selected by General Guisan as chief of the general staff to replace Corps Commander Jakob Labhart on

January 1, 1940. Labhart had occupied this post for many years, but Guisan found that operational planning in view of an impending conflict had been neglected, did not like Labhart for his pro-German leanings, and was looking for somebody with whom he could cooperate. This did not prevent General Guisan from giving Labhart the command of an army corps and promising to reinstate him as chief of staff at the end of the war. It was a typical Swiss decision, as in Switzerland error is easily forgiven when committed in high places and sanctions are practically never taken, even when a man has been a failure. It was also a compromise solution, since President Pilet-Golaz had come to the defense of Labhart. Only strong intervention by Federal Councillor Minger had convinced the government that it had to approve the change desired by the general if it wanted to avoid the general's resignation.

Jakob Huber, the new chief whom Guisan appreciated because he was so different from him, was an engineer and a professional soldier. He had introduced modern methods of target acquisition, command, and control for the artillery. I remembered him from one weekend when I was a boy when he briefed my father, then a captain, on indirect fire control in a field battery. When not teaching and instructing, Huber was not given to talking. He had married the daughter of the owner of one of the old large inns still existing on the roads to the alpine passes, an elegant and witty woman who liked to talk. This permitted him to wrap himself in deep silence. During professional discussions he used to listen without uttering so much as a word. At the end he generally gave the right solution in one short, superbly formulated sentence.

In this extremely critical period of the war, a small group of officers, most of them from the intelligence service and the general staff, got together and formed a kind of conspiracy. In the positions they held, they were acutely aware of the defeatism spread by some high-ranking officers and influential politicians. They probably did not know well enough the basic and stubborn will of the overwhelming majority of the officers and the rank and file of the armed forces to resist at any cost, a frame of mind poles removed from the mood of some politicians and the habit of appeasement cultivated by the minister of foreign affairs. The idea to form a conspiratorial group was conceived toward the end of June – was it under the influence of de Gaulle's famous resistance speech of June 18, 1940? – and the group was formally founded at a meeting in Lucerne in the middle of July, when the members pledged to not obey orders implying surrender and to prevent commanders from giving such orders. Before they were able to set up a real network in the army, the movement, about which too many had talked, was uncovered. Since initially there was the suspicion that it was pro-German, its members were arrested on August 3. The truth soon was established, however, that they were pursuing patriotic aims in all sincerity. Notwithstanding, they had to be punished for attempted insubordination, but this was done in a symbolic and extremely lenient way. The fifteen leaders were summoned to appear before the general. He admonished them, yet assured them of his entire confidence, and they then shook hands.[14]

The "insurrection" was thus liquidated, never to raise its head again. It had outlived its extremely short life and probably had been unnecessary, since it is unlikely, given the tradition of discipline deep-rooted in the Swiss officer, that even officers with personal pro-German leanings would not have done their duty. One of the most controversial men, Divisional Commander Eugen Bircher, once said to me in 1941 during one of his visits to Berlin, "If attacked, we will perform great feats of arms, but finally will be defeated."

General Guisan had the next word after the president's enigmatic and ominous speech. He asked the government, formally, whether his mission to protect the country militarily subsisted in the changed strategic environment. This was emphatically confirmed by the Federal Council. However, the government stuck to its earlier decision to order a partial demobilization of the army. On July 7, the number of men under arms was reduced to 200,000, and later to 150,000. Those remaining now needed guidance and new motivation. Therefore, on July 2, the general had issued an order of the day, the central part of which was, "An armistice is not peace. The war continues between Germany, Italy, and Great Britain. . . . Even if we cannot win a direct victory, we will fight."[15]

The country and the people, in the meantime, were getting no official guidance and continued in a state of bewilderment, veering between defeatism and grim determination. The Swiss partisans of Germany now saw their chance. Their motives varied. Some were simply scared and wanted to appease the German colossus, some thought that it would be good for business if Switzerland were completely integrated into the economic straitjacket of the German war economy, which the Germans euphemistically called "New Europe." Others had always disliked free institutions and a free press and now saw a chance to destroy these liberties. Some were traditionally pro-German and admired everything coming from north of the Rhine. Some saw a chance of replacing a system of government that they considered too democratic with a more authoritarian system—which at that time seemed in fashion. Some belonged to the lunatic fringe. They all were encouraged by agents skillfully infiltrated into Switzerland. Among them was a certain Klaus Hügel, who posed as the chairman of the chamber of commerce in Stuttgart and under this disguise was especially successful. In reality he was a high-ranking officer in the Gestapo's spy organization, under SS General Schellenberg, and also in close cooperation with Goebbels's Propaganda Ministry in Berlin. Hügel succeeded in holding conferences with leading Swiss businessmen, conferences that were even welcomed by Swiss officials around Pilet-Golaz. He talked freely with church leaders, members of the press, and business leaders. At least four of these meetings were reported between 1940 and 1942, and many a Swiss participant thought he was serving his country well by appeasing influential German circles.

The National Socialist subversion, combined with the propaganda directed toward the workers by the left-wing Socialists and the Communists—Stalin's Soviet Union was still an ally of Germany—now began to bear fruit. As we have seen, small groups of the bourgeoisie—some because of their pro-German leanings, others because of their business interests or their general antiliberal attitudes—had been receptive to

Hitler's and Goebbels's propaganda. Now the slogan that Hitler's Germany was abolishing capitalism began to filter down to the rank and file of the manual work force. Several socialist newspapers, which up to now had strongly opposed National Socialism, suddenly discovered the Nazis' achievements in the interest of the so-called working class. The assertion that in Germany work and high salaries were guaranteed from now on made a deep impression on the manual worker. Some believed that social security for the soldier was better taken care of by Hitler than by the Swiss democratic institutions. The peasants were told that in Germany interest on loans was abolished, which confirmed many of them in their admiration for Germany and its widely advertised efforts to further peasantry as the basis of a nation's health.[16]

The most significant – if not really effective – result of the defeatism and discouragement that spread after the defeat of France and the withdrawal of the British to their islands was that a small group of men conceived the idea that it was now their business to inaugurate a new policy. They sent a petition to the Federal Council, outlining in eight points a policy of appeasement and collaboration with Germany. The petition initially was signed by a historian, a Protestant minister, a private banker, a retired professional officer, an industrialist, a schoolteacher, and a leader in the insurance business. Ninety-eight others from all walks of life signed after them. The paper was sent to the government on November 15, 1940, backed up until April 1941 by additional signatures, which finally totaled 173. The paper later became famous, or infamous, under the name "Petition of the Two Hundred." The main points of the document were the proposals to abolish freedom of the press, to take sanctions against some editors, and to revoke court sentences already pronounced for treasonable acts in favor of Germany.[17]

The petition, with its illegal demands, was of course rejected by the government, and criminal investigations were started against its authors, yet were soon dropped. The full text was not published at the time, but what had become known had an effect totally opposite to the intentions of the petition's authors: The press and the vast majority of the Swiss were outraged. A typical cartoon in a newspaper showed a man scratching his head and asking, "Now, am I a fool or am I a scoundrel?" The will to resist German infiltration and German arrogance was strengthened.

CHAPTER FOUR

Fortress Switzerland

The Birth of an Idea

The Army Position, organized and fortified during the winter of 1939/40, was designed to resist an onslaught from the north between the Austrian border and the end of the Maginot Line. Military planning had to take into account all possible contingencies, and the general staff studied, among other problems, situations that would develop if the Germans broke through the Army Position.

This possibility had also been considered in the ultrasecret exchanges with the French supreme command and discussed with its representative, Lieutenant Colonel Garteiser, during his frequent visits to a possible future theater of operations in the area between the Alps and the Jura. The most likely solution seemed then – long before the German offensive of May 1940 – to be a strong French position somewhere across Switzerland, facing east. What would remain of the Swiss army could fall back onto that position.[1]

Another possibility considered was that the Swiss forces, when forced back from their Army Position, would withdraw in a southerly direction into the Alps and there make their last stand.[2] Consequently, staff studies commissioned by the general and the chief of the general staff also included the problems involved in a withdrawal to the center of the Alps. The officers mainly entrusted with these special studies were Colonel Alfred Strüby, in civilian life an agricultural engineer; Colonel Oscar A. Germann, a professor of law; and Lieutenant Colonel Samuel Gonard, a professional artillery

officer. Their various proposals had much in common insofar
as they conceived of a central position around the St. Gotthard massif, commanding the strategically important transit
routes across the Alps. They only differed as to the extent and
the shape of the area to be definitively held.[3]

The role of what would remain of the Swiss army after a
defeat in the Army Position would be that of defending a
reduced stronghold, in which the government could survive
on national soil as a symbol of continued national existence.
The example of the Belgians and their king, holding out from
1914 to 1918 in the northwestern corner of their country,
was, of course, very much present in the planners' minds.
From this stronghold the left wing of the Germans, which
would be confronted somewhere in western Switzerland by
the French, would be harassed and threatened. All this planning, of course, was based on the assumption of a protracted
1914/18–style war between Germany and France, without
the participation of Italy. After the collapse of France and
once Italy became Germany's partner and ally in the war,
everything appeared in a completely new light. The plan of a
central position in the Alps, a National Redoubt or *réduit national*, which had already been proposed, now gathered a
new and different significance.

On the night of June 24/25, 1940, the very night when the
armistice between Germany and France came into force,
General Guisan met the chief of the general staff, Corps Commander Jakob Huber, and some of the staff officers involved
in contingency planning. The general had decided already to
concentrate the main forces on the defense of a National
Redoubt; the question was now to decide on its shape and
precise location. Huber presented a map with a rough sketch
of the possible distribution of forces. This sketch, with
amendments made by the general and with specific instructions as to details, now became the basis of complex staff
work. Out of it sprang Operations Order No. 12, which was
in the hands of the corps commanders on July 20. Prelim-
inary orders had already set in motion a part of the armed
forces toward the new area to be held.[4]

The plan was a simple one. The army was to occupy a position at the foot of the mountain chain stretching from the fortress of Sargans in the east to the fortress St. Maurice in the west. It is the line where the Alps begin to rise from the lowlands, called the plateau. In addition to this, a southern line had to be held so that the southern and northern lines together would form an ellipse surrounding the whole central alpine area. The southern position followed the very high mountain chains—including the Matterhorn—that form the frontier with Italy. The ellipse included at its center the fortified area around the St. Gotthard Pass, a number of deep and wide valleys with small industrial cities, and a number of already existing underground storehouses for fuel and ammunition. About a quarter of the total population of the country lived in this area. In the north of the oval, an advanced line—including the already existing Army Position, which in the meantime had been extended far to the west—was to be occupied. This advanced position formed a wide arc that was fortified, but only thinly manned. Its mission was to slow down an eventual German attack against the redoubt.[5]

The political and psychological implications of this plan were momentous. It meant abandoning not less than half of the national territory, three-quarters of the population, and all the larger cities—including the federal capital, Berne—to an invader. Lieutenant Colonel Gonard had read his *Peloponnesian War* by Thucydides, as I learned in many an animated discussion with him when (a few years later) he had become an army corps commander and I served on his staff. So he knew of course Pericles's speech to the Athenians in which he said, when the territory of Attica was threatened to be laid waste by the Spartans: "If only I could persuade you to come forward from your city and to destroy your own possessions in these outlying territories, so as to show the Peloponnesians that your concern for those things cannot be used by them to exert pressure on you."[6]

The military planners did not seem to doubt for a minute that the people would accept their tragic decision. They were convinced that only a show of real strength and determination would give them a chance of avoiding invasion and war. In view of the extremely far-reaching nature of the

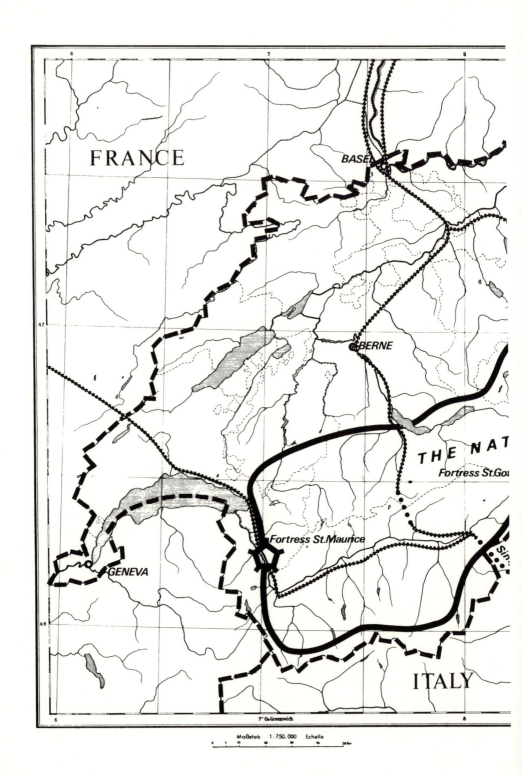

FRANCE

BASEL

BERNE

THE NAT

Fortress St.Go

Fortress St.Maurice

GENEVA

Sim

ITALY

7°0 Greenwich

Maßstab 1 : 750.000 Echelle

0 5 10 20 30 40 50 Km

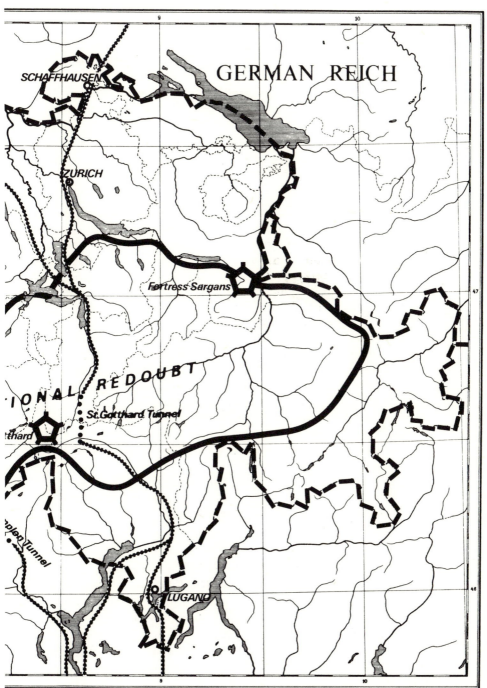

SCHAFFHAUSEN

GERMAN REICH

ZURICH

Fortress Sargans

ONAL REDOUBT

St.Gotthard Tunnel

thard

plen Tunnel

LUGANO

decision, the general addressed a long note on July 12, 1940, to the head of the military department, Minister of Defense and Federal Councillor Rudolf Minger, in which he stated his decision, the new plan of defense, and the motives that had guided him and his advisers toward the new strategy.

The new strategy outlined in this document is the classical example of deterrence, or dissuasion, and was formulated by the general as follows:

> While Germany and Italy, as long as they have not broken England's resistance, certainly have no interest in adding new conflicts to the existing one, it has to be assumed that the direct communication lines across our Alps are of great importance to them, at least to the first-named power. This power, therefore, might be tempted to exert pressures against Switzerland — economic, political, even military — with the aim of gaining free disposal of these transit lines.
>
> Under the existing circumstances the German impositions might become such as to be no longer compatible with our independence and our national honor. Switzerland can only avoid the threat of a direct German attack if the German high command, while preparing such an attack, becomes convinced that a war against us would be long and costly, that it would create a new battleground in the heart of Europe, in a most useless and dangerous way, and thus jeopardize the realization of its other plans.
>
> The aim and principle of our national defense, from now on, therefore, has to be to show to our neighbors that such a war would be a long and costly enterprise.[7]

There were, and still are, of course, people who did not understand and do not understand the full meaning of this strategy. They protested. The government acquiesced. The people and the army — which became familiar with its meaning, its essence, and its full implications only step by step as it executed its new mission — accepted. They felt, with the wisdom of human beings who draw their strength from the deepest roots of tradition, that the National Redoubt was their only hope of salvation.[8]

Guisan at the Rütli

No sooner was the decision taken than the general instructed his personal staff to prepare for a secret meeting of all commanding officers, without exception – from corps commanders down to battalion commanders, whether mobilized or at home. On July 18, they received orders to report a week later at a certain point in Lucerne.

There, at the pier facing the station, a lake steamer was waiting, surrounded by armed motor launches and a battalion of mountain infantry. All the officers who had been summoned were present and boarded the ship. Some thought then, and some said later, that it was unwise to have all the COs in the same boat. Yet the genenal's men had calculated the risk and knew what they were doing. Soon, the boat reached the entrance of the narrowest part of the Lake of Lucerne, where it looks like a Norwegian fjord and is surrounded by almost vertical cliffs. At the foot of one of these sheer cliffs is a grassy slope, surrounded by thick woods, called the Rütli. It was here, on this meadow, on August 1, 1291, that the Swiss Confederation was founded. For a Swiss patriot it is a holy ground.[9]

At this historical spot the 650 officers gathered around General Guisan. He spoke to them, in German with his heavy French accent, from a few penciled notes (now lost). In his hand he held a few letters addressed to him from simple citizens and schoolchildren, and he quoted from them. At the center of his short speech – of which no verbatim record was taken – the general said, according to a later official hand-out:

In 1939 the Federal Council entrusted the army with the task of protecting our centuries-old independence. This independence has been respected, until now, by our neighbors, and we will see to it that it will be respected to the end. As long as in Europe millions stand under arms, and as long as important forces are able to attack us at any time, the army has to remain at its post.

Come what may, the fortifications you have built preserve all their value. Our efforts have not been in vain, since we still hold our destiny in our own hands. Don't listen to those who, out of ignorance or evil intention, spread negative news and doubt. Let us trust not only in our right but also in our strength, which enables us, if everybody is possessed of an iron will, to defend ourselves successfully.

On August 1 you will fully realize that the new positions that I have ordered you to occupy are those in which your arms and your courage in the new situation will be most effective for the defense and the good of the country.

After the address, an order of the day was handed to the officers, to be read by the commanders to the troops. The people learned of the gathering on the following Sunday night by radio and in the press in a short official communiqué in which an extract of the general's speech, as translated above, of only 17 lines (120 words) was included.[10]

However, the news of the Rütli spread, details became known, and the effect was immediate and electrifying. Pilet-Golaz's unfortunate speech receded into the shadow. The movements of the army into their fresh positions were well under way; the building of fortifications had begun in the interior of the country. Everybody could see that a new chapter had begun. Hope of being able to withstand even increased pressures by the Axis powers spread far and wide.

The Germans, on learning of the general's appeal and order of the day, were furious. Did he imply, since he spoke of millions able to attack Switzerland, that Germany might plan an assault? The hope that Switzerland would now go the Austrian way and become a docile member of the so-called New Europe, which Berlin had begun to propagate and already presented as a reality, had suddenly been shattered, and the National Socialists resented it bitterly.

The moral crisis that had swept the country carried General Guisan to the top of his popularity. Even a deeply democratic people needs leadership in time of crisis, leadership visibly represented by a human being. Remember the mythological figure of William Tell! The Federal Council, a committee of seven, because of its very constitutional weakness and also because of the lack of fortitude of most of its members, could never satisfy this profound need. The desire to see the country's aspirations represented by one man was strengthened by the political trend of those years, which had seen so many dictators rise to the top. Therefore, from the day of his election, General Guisan had become a symbol, to many a father figure. Now, after the Rütli where he had rallied the army around a new task and instilled new confidence in its commanders, where he had redressed the harm done by the president of the confederation with his speech of June 25, Guisan had become the embodiment of the nation's hopes.

Needless to say such an extraordinary position in the eyes of the people, a position rarely attained by a Swiss and in opposition to the tradition, did not fail to produce deep conflicts with the political leadership, whose ego was hurt by the preeminence of the general. The Federal Council went so far as to discuss, shortly after the Rütli appeal, the possibility of officially ending the active service of the army, a step that automatically would also have ended the mission of the commander-in-chief.[11] This plan, however, was soon dropped, since it was too much in opposition with the mood of the country.

For General Guisan the burden of his responsibility in the later months of 1940 had become almost intolerable. He did not receive any encouragement from the Federal Council, his immediate superior, but rather sensed the sullen opposition of those of its seven members who were his enemies. He also knew that his best friend in the government, Rudolf Minger, had decided to resign in December. One of the reasons for this unexpected resignation probably was Minger's involvement in the secret arrangements with the French high command in 1939 and Minger's sense that his involvement was a great danger for the country.[12] How far Guisan shared this feeling is difficult to say, but it certainly added to his burden.

The general was deeply conscious of the fact that he had opted for a strategy that would entail, in the case of a German attack, the loss of large portions of the country and would bring a large proportion of the population under the domination of the National Socialist terror regime. On the other hand, he felt the overwhelming confidence that the people, blindly, had put in him. They trusted him to protect them. Yet, was the strategy of the National Redoubt, hardly initiated, a sufficient guarantee? He knew that it was not. The country was now surrounded by the Axis powers and their armies. Stalin's Soviet Union was Germany's ally. With it at his side, Hitler could dominate the whole of Europe. The only power resisting this colossal agglomeration of power was Great Britain, on faraway islands reeling under the German bombing attack. For Guisan, it was essential to avert war in this moment, when all odds were against Switzerland.

Guisan now learned of plans (inspired by the example of Sweden's sending Sven Hedin, the famous explorer and admirer of German imperialism) to visit Hitler and implore his benevolence. According to these plans, Switzerland also should start a diplomatic offensive to win German forbearance. According to the authors of the plans, certain Swiss personalities might be able, by personal contact, to appease Hitler and explore ways of coexisting with Germany in its New Europe, without losing national independence. Such ideas, originating in pro-German circles in the army or with influential opportunists in the business world, and also endorsed by politicians and even members of the Federal Council, now became the order of day. Pilet-Golaz, the foreign minister, opposed them however. He did not think that anybody but himself should or could deal with the dreaded Germans.

Some thought that a former president of the confederation, Edmund Schulthess, who had been minister for economic affairs for not less than twenty-four years (from 1912 to 1935), a kind of Salazar and a Germanophile, was the right man for the negotiations. Others proposed Carl J. Burckhardt, a former high commissioner of the League of Nations in Danzig from 1937 to 1939 and now a leading officer of the Red Cross. Burckhardt himself did not know of the plan, and certainly would not have approved it, which shows how unrealistic it was. It was unrealistic also in the sense that Hitler would not have received and listened to any Swiss emissary at that time. Actually, none of these missions ever materialized.

In this tense atmosphere – in which some ducked for cover, others relished in self-accusation, still others produced plans and ideas for appeasing the Germans without losing national independence, and only a few voices advocating a cool distance from the so-called New Europe could be heard – General Guisan made a most unusual move, which he himself later regretted. Influenced by men close to him and under the heavy pressures that have been described, he sent, on August 14, 1940, a long letter to Federal Councillor Minger.

The incredible document proposed an "embassy" to Berlin by a "new man," and warmly recommended Carl J. Burckhardt. The argument for Burckhardt revealed at once that the idea was not Guisan's own. His advisers had convinced him that he, being a *Suisse romand*, could not understand the new Germanic civilization and the new cultural trends represented by the Third Reich, or what was good in it, and that, therefore, a man of "essentially Germanic culture," Burckhardt, had to initiate a new "policy of prestige and propaganda" for Switzerland. (Burckhardt had been a professor of history at the University of Zurich and at the Graduate Institute for International Studies in Geneva, and was the author of works on French – not German – history. In connection with his difficult mission as high commissioner in Danzig, he had met Hitler on August 11, 1939.) Another of the naive and preposterous proposals in the general's letter was to win the support of Count Volpi di Misurata, a former Fascist minister of finance, in order to establish, via Italy, closer relations with the United States. The letter also contained the ominous words "appeasement" and "collaboration."[13]

Guisan's letter was in absolute contradication to his thinking as we know it. He always had avoided meddling in diplomatic and political affairs, and now he came forward with a dozen different ideas for a diplomatic offensive! He always had stood for determination and military resistance, and now he advocated appeasement! The only explanation we can give is that some men he trusted had abused his friendship and kindness and inspired – nay, dictated – the letter.

Old Rudolf Minger, after receiving the document, did the only reasonable thing: he let it disappear in a drawer, never mentioning it to anybody. When, much later, it was published, it tarnished the image of General Guisan but did not otherwise do any harm.

The National Redoubt

Although Fortress Switzerland, the National Redoubt, was becoming an ever-stronger reality, many tactical and operational amendments, based on new experiences and studies, had to be added to the original plan. The first line of defense, closely following the national border on all sides, was maintained. Until the end it was to be of great strategic value for several reasons: it was based on a chain of permanent fortifications and strong natural and artifical obstacles, and it was manned by soldiers living on the spot. Its mission was to give the population a certain sense of being protected, and to delay an invader until the planned demolitions could be made and the army mobilized to full strength.

The second advanced line mentioned, the semicircle originally based on the extended Army Position, soon had to be evacuated. The experiences of the countries that were at war seemed to prove that with the reduced forces now available this advanced position could not be held for any length of time. The campaign in Russia demonstrated the enormously increased firepower of modern armies; dispersion in two successive positions now seemed doomed to failure; and a concentration of all available forces in the alpine redoubt seemed therefore advisable. The divisions that became available after the advanced semicircle was evacuated were assigned tasks within the national fortress.

As we have seen, the central position was selected because of the high mountain chains surrounding it. They were and are practically inaccessible for armored vehicles. Yet these mountain chains are crossed by deep valleys at at least seven points, which became known as the "doors to the *réduit.*" The forces now available were mainly moved to these points, and forts with heavy artillery were installed at these "doors." In the interior of the redoubt the railroads needed additional defenses. In valleys where airborne troops might land, special defensive forces were stationed – light artillery, anti-aircraft artillery, and motorized troops.

The National Redoubt had become a real fortress – under one condition: that it would be possible to mobilize early enough all the necessary troops not yet under arms and to move them into their prepared positions in the Alps before an attack began.

However, in the course of the war, defense strategy was elastically adapted to the changing situations. As soon as an attack from all directions became less likely, say by the summer of 1942, the defense of the national territory in its totality was again envisaged. Forces began to move again across the plateau and toward the borders, regaining, in the process, their mobility and their spirit of enterprise. On September 1, 1942, the order of operations W42 was issued,[14] designed to oppose an encircling movement of the Allies through France and Switzerland against the south of Germany. After the American-British-Canadian landing in Normandy on June 6, 1944, the possibility of an Allied attack through Switzerland in the course of a turning movement around the southern end of the Siegfried Line became a probability and a serious preoccupation. We know that Marshal Stalin strongly advocated such an action.

Concern was serious indeed. Such an attack by the Allies would have forced Switzerland into an intolerable situation. The Swiss high command was determined to oppose such an attack, according to the duties of a neutral nation. But, at the same time, it prepared to oppose a German intervention as well. It would have been politically impossible and unthinkable to accept German assistance and thereby become an ally and belligerent on the hated National Socialist side. Plans were laid for opposing any German attempt to penetrate Swiss territory under the pretext of fighting an Allied advance across Switzerland. The prospect was war on two fronts or rather two separate wars, one against the Allies and one against the Germans.

A German-Italian Attack?

For economic and political reasons it was possible to keep, on average, only a fourth of the army's effective strength permanently under arms. The high command had to rely on being able to remobilize the rest at short notice. This fast mobilization was carefully prepared for and rehearsed time and time again. Yet it was, of course, essential to know when to mobilize so as not to be surprised by an attack. Military intelligence, therefore, became an essential element of Swiss defensive strategy. On it depended the timely occupation of the positions in the Alps. Under this pressure, the intelligence service gradually developed into a very sensitive instrument, sometimes recording nonexistent threats. The Germans and the Allies were not long in discovering this. By leaking false information they could now force the Swiss to increase their defensive measures, and both sides did leak such information. All military threats registered in the course of the war also have to be considered from this angle.

The question must be asked and answered, Was there at any time in the war a real threat of a German-Italian attack? The Swiss thought so at different moments. Since the effect of their defensive effort depended so much on an early warning of impending danger, even minute hints had to be taken seriously. One had to be on the lookout for any ominous signs. There was one example of such a hardly visible, yet sinister sign in August 1942, when the Germans, in the midst of their operations deep inside the Soviet Union, were confronted with serious transport problems. Berlin instructed its military attaché in Berne to find out and report how many heavy trucks existed in Switzerland.[15] This special bit of information did not call for any particular precaution, but it generally added to the deep gloom that characterized that period. It was the time of the German summer offensive in Russia, which reached the Volga on August 23, 1942, and of Rommel's offensive in North Africa, which led him into Egypt.

We have extensively described the alarm of May 1940 and know that the threat then was only a ruse of the Germans. This does not, of course, preclude the possibility that an attack against Switzerland could have been launched at any moment, especially after the fall of France. The German forces were on the spot, and it evidently depended only on Hitler's strategic inspiration how his obedient and well-trained instrument of war was used.

Not only were the German forces available, operation plans also had been prepared. They are known in all their details. On the day of the armistice between Germany and France, planning began in Berlin under the code name "Operation Tannenbaum." The study was completed by German Army Group C and sent, on October 7, 1940, to the general staff. It made provision for twenty-one divisions, including some Italian forces, for operations against Switzerland. The *Wehrmachtführungsstab* (chiefs of staff) found the study unrealistic and gave orders for a new one to take its place, using only half the number of divisions. Today it is evident that the whole study was only an exercise in strategic and operational planning and that there was never any serious intention of carrying it out.[16]

Another study, by a former Austrian officer then in the SS, a certain Colonel Boehme, was made in December 1943 for implementation in the summer of 1944. His idea was to have a surprise attack against Switerland by fifteen divisions from all four sides. Boehme's plan was even more amateurish than the former Tannenbaum; none of these plans seems to have been taken seriously by those in positions of responsibility, and all remained pigeonholed.[17]

Much more interesting was a remark written down by a serious soldier, General Franz Halder, chief of the German general staff until September 1942. On October 6, 1940, he noted in his diary, when he was driving along the Swiss border from Germany into France: "The border area of the Jura offers no favorable base for an attack. Switzerland rises, in successive waves of wood-covered terrain, across the axis of an attack. The crossing points on the river Doubs and the border are few; the Swiss frontier position is strong."[18]

On March 19, 1943 – at the time the Germans expected the Allied landing in Italy – the Viking line of the Swiss military intelligence, which led right up into the German high command, informed Berne that the Germans were now considering an action against Switzerland. Similar information was planted in Stockholm. From Munich came news of a concentration of mountain troops in Bavaria and the presence of General Eduard Dietl, a famous mountain warfare specialist.

(Dietl was actually in Finland at the time.) A week after this alarming information, which had come from various sources, it was learned through the same channels that the danger had passed. It certainly had not only passed, it had never existed; the signals had been given in order to ensure that the Swiss did not diminish their mobilized strength, which at that time was about 170,000. In Berlin this strength was thought to be the minimum force possible to convince the Allies that it would be unwise to plan, in the course of their impending advance through Italy, any operation across Switzerland against Germany's "soft underbelly."[19]

It was at the same time in 1943 that trade negotiations with Germany were conducted in an especially bitter atmosphere. The Swiss, favored by the military successes of the Allies, had begun to reduce their exports to Germany and to limit credit. It is not quite impossible that the one-week military threat in March was intended, perhaps by some very junior official, to lend a helping hand to Berlin's negotiators.

If we know today that the fear of a German-Italian military attack was exaggerated or even unfounded, we also know that the situation would have been completely different if the Swiss had not been ready to fight. Hitler himself, involved as he was at that time in his world-shattering strategic fantasies, had never given Switzerland more than a passing thought. As for the Italians, they would never have been able to overcome the border defenses without German help—not to speak of the formidable fortresses in the Alps—and they knew it.

Railroads Through the Alps

The main axes connecting western and central Europe with Italy are the international railroad links of Mont Cenis (France-Italy), Simplon (Switzerland-Italy), St. Gotthard (Switzerland-Italy), and Brenner (Germany-Austria-Italy). In 1940, when Italy joined the German Reich in its adventure of conquest, the railroads across the Alps became of primordial strategic importance. The British sea blockade, of course, made any maritime transport between the two Axis powers impossible. The Mont Cenis, connecting the French railroad network with northern Italy, was too eccentric to be of great importance. Simplon and St. Gotthard, crossing the territory of a neutral power, could not be used for military transport. Therefore, besides the Tauern line linking Salzburg with Trieste and Venice, virtually only the Brenner rail link remained to carry German troops and arms to Italy and eventually Italian forces and war stores to Germany.

In order to enable the railroads in Axis hands to carry this heavy strategic traffic, the Germans and Italians had to rely completely on the Simplon and St. Gotthard for transport of what was loosely termed nonstrategic goods: coal, steel, oil, timber, wheat for Italy, and agricultural products for Germany. Such traffic was entrusted to the Swiss railroads on the basis of an international treaty of October 13, 1909, concluded with Italy and Germany, obliging Switzerland to admit for regular transportation all goods except war materials. The Swiss always quoted the clauses of this treaty to the Allies when they asked for this traffic to be reduced.[20]

The Swiss railroads, electrified and with ultramodern equipment, were able to handle the enormous exchange of these goods. For the Allies, of course, this service given to the enemy was the cause of passionate objections and was a source of constant conflict, especially between Berne and Washington. For the Germans, this traffic across neutral land on fast and undamaged lines was of great, if indirect, strategic value. It meant the Mont Cenis and Brenner lines could be devoted exclusively to military transport. Yet this also caused the Axis powers concern, since it made them dependent on Switzerland. The Swiss, theoretically, could interrupt this traffic at any time. For the Swiss, the railroads across the Alps were a powerful weapon in their negotiations with the Axis powers about the vital supplies on which Switzerland depended entirely for its independent survival. Berne did not consider interrupting this traffic totally, less out of fear that Germany would forcibly attempt to seize the railroads than because Switzerland needed them as a means of extracting from Germany concessions that otherwise would not have been made. We will show, in the next chapters, how dramatic Switzerland's dependence on outside supplies was and how little choice it had in its relations with the belligerents.

The railways through the Alps were also fully integrated as a weapon into the new strategy of the Fortress Switzerland, the alpine redoubt organized at the beginning of July 1940. The railway tunnels of the Simplon (twenty kilometers long) and the St. Gotthard (fifteen kilometers long) had, from the outset, been prepared for demolition. Large explosive charges could be placed in chambers hewn in the rock. The accesses to the tunnels and the sites to be eventually blown up were protected by permanent fortifications, some of which had been built at the time the railroads were constructed. Now, in 1940, additional demolitions were prepared for installation on the feeder lines.

The danger that the Germans might try, by a sudden invasion, to get control of the vital railroad system to prevent its destruction could not be ignored. On the other hand, there was also the risk that the Allies, by air raids and sabotage, might try to interrupt these arteries because they were so vital for the enemy. Therefore, tactical measures had to be taken both for protecting the lines and for guaranteeing the planned demolitions if the situation became that extreme. The tracks and vulnerable objects such as the countless bridges, tunnels, and high-tension cables were heavily guarded and, moreover, surrounded by strong outer defenses. Antiaircraft artillery was positioned all along the lines. Strategically the National Redoubt was so designed as to include the vital crossings of the Alps and to defend all accesses to them. By so doing, the Swiss automatically added to the *réduit*'s outer defenses the immensely strong deterrent effect of the possibility of blowing up the railroads, making them unserviceable for years.

To make this instrument of deterrence effective, the army's resolution to destroy the railroads rather than to let them fall into the hands of an invader had to be made thoroughly known. General Guisan used every possible occasion to emphasize this strategy. When he met with the head of German espionage against Switzerland, General Walter Schellenberg, on March 3, 1943 (a meeting that is discussed further in a later chapter), he stated unmistakably and in strong words his determination to demolish the transit lines in case of a German attack.

In this way the railroads across the Alps played a double role throughout the war – they were part of the strategic deterrent as well as a weapon in the difficult economic negotiations with the Axis powers. The Swiss government successfully resisted all German attempts to forward noncivilian goods – unlike Sweden where even troops, although without their arms, were allowed across the neutral country. It would have been impossible to carry any war materials across Switzerland clandestinely, since the trains were closely examined by the customs guards and even more closely by a network of spies that the American legation in Berne had recruited, mostly from the many Italian refugees residing in Switzerland.

Yet even the "civilian" transports were considered strategic in their final effect, especially by the Americans, and quite understandably so. They were "strategic" because they freed the railroads in German hands from a great mass of heavy traffic, and it is difficult anyway to deny that things such as oil and steel are of strategic importance. In June 1943 the British and the U.S. governments requested that the Swiss not accept any more shipments of oil between Germany and Italy. The reply was that since the Allies had cut the oil supply to the Swiss entirely, they were now dependent on oil from Romania, which was only delivered by Germany as long as Italy's share of the oil was carried by them across Switzerland. In August 1944 the request was repeated and extended to all kinds of goods even though, in March 1944, the Swiss, while resisting the demands, had unilaterally reduced the amounts carried to the levels that had been carried before the war.

The Americans never accepted the distinction between strategic and civilian supplies, which in modern total war is obsolete and meaningless indeed. They also were unable to see the strategic problem that existed for Switzerland. They saw only one side, namely, that a neutral was "helping the enemy," and not the other side, that the neutral had to extract concessions from that very enemy in order to survive and had to use every instrument at its disposal for this purpose. The Americans never recognized the remarkable fact that during the four years when Switzerland was wholly enclosed by Axis territory, it made so few concessions to the Axis powers.[21]

The British showed more comprehension, since they had great experience in handling blockades and waging economic war for political ends, whereas for Washington it was total war and total war alone. Thus the rocks of the St. Gotthard became a kind of dividing line, where moral and legal rights and views about neutrals and a neutral's moral and legal rights and duties met and confronted each other.

CHAPTER FIVE

The War Economy

Early Preparations

Switzerland is a small and densely populated country – surface 41,300 square kilometers, population (at the time we are writing about) 4.2 million, which means more than 100 people per square kilometer – and depends for its bare existence on imports of food and raw materials, for which it has to pay by exporting manufactured goods, providing the services of its banks and insurance companies, and attracting tourists to enjoy its natural beauties. In the thirties the imports of industrial raw materials and foodstuffs amounted to 7.5 million tons per year, including 1.2 million tons from overseas.

In the years of growing tension that preceded the Second World War, it was fully recognized how vulnerable a country that depended so much on foreign trade would be in case of a new European war. Preparations for organizing the economy for such a contingency began as early as 1937. On April 1, 1938, legislation was enacted to secure the production and importation of essential commodities. From then on, permits for importing certain goods were granted only to those firms that pledged themselves to hold enough stock for at least six months. The federal government itself acquired considerable reserves of wheat and sugar for consumption by the army. Later, when the threat of an invasion increased, it was ordered that these stores be brought to the alpine valleys in the center of the country.

The agriculture of Switzerland, at that time, had concentrated on milk and dairy products as well as meat, the traditional stock-in-trade of the country. There was only a small surface devoted to growing wheat. Sixty percent of the wheat consumed, 85 percent of the sugar, 50 percent of the fats and oils, and, of course, 100 percent of the coffee, tea, and cocoa were imported. In the food sector the country was only self-sufficient in regard to potatoes and vegetables.

In the beginning of April 1939, a whole series of laws were enacted that were to prove beneficial in the coming years. The farmers were instructed to treble the surface for wheat from 1,000 to 3,000 square kilometers, while it was recognized that 5,000 square kilometers would be necessary to meet the country's needs.

A shadow organization was now set up to run the country's war economy. It enlisted the support of every single township and every canton (state) of the confederation and also utilized experienced and specialized private organizations for specific tasks. The whole effort was directed by high officials of the federal administration and by men and women recruited from private enterprise who served on a "militia" basis, most of the time without pay.[1] The task of this new organization was to control the use of all raw materials and to distribute them among the individual firms according to their importance for the war effort and the survival of the population.

In the framework of the new organization for securing the functioning of the economy in case of war, provision had to be made for maintaining the sea transport of the 1.2 million tons of goods needed every year. Fifteen Greek steamers were chartered in the London market. In addition, the government bought several small freighters totaling 60,000 tons. A general agent was installed in London with special powers for supervising the operations of the ships, chartered and owned. Port commissioners were appointed for Genoa, Lisbon, and Marseilles, and their tasks were to speed up the unloading of consignments for Switzerland, to fight red tape, and to organize transportation over land. Special representatives in New York (later in Baltimore and Philadelphia as well), Madrid, Cerbère (where goods are transshipped from the Spanish railroads to the French trains), and Istanbul were to take care of the many formalities involved in the shipment, transshipment, and forwarding of supplies to Switzerland. A special agent was even delegated to Berlin to deal with the problems created by the German counterblockade and by submarine warfare.

Two years after the outbreak of the war, the landlocked country, curiously enough, enacted a maritime law of its own. Basel was designated as the Swiss seaport, seagoing vessels were registered there, and now the ships' captains were authorized to fly the red flag with the white cross on the high seas.

Food is Rationed

Just before the outbreak of the war the preparatory work achieved by the new organization made itself dramatically felt. On April 4, 1939, an appeal had been issued to the whole population to stockpile food for at least two months. In case of war, it was pointed out, no food except bread, milk, and vegetables would be sold. Poor people who could not afford the expense of acquiring such a reserve were issued "blue cards" that would permit them to buy their daily provisions normally.

On August 28, 1939, when war was imminent, all sales from a long list of foodstuffs, including sugar and oil, were stopped for two months. Exceptions were made for those households holding a "blue card." After a two months' embargo, rationing of essentials took effect on October 30, 1939. Every household had by now received its ration cards.

After the defeat of France, the country was totally encircled by the Axis powers, the food situation grew serious, and a new two-month embargo was ordered. Beginning October 1940, all edible fats were rationed, and gradually, as the situation grew worse, rationing began to include such commodities as coffee, tea, cocoa, cheese, eggs, meat, and (beginning October 16, 1942) bread. Milk, chocolate, and even dog food were to follow. From 1944 on, potato flour was rationed as well as bread. On two days every week all consumption of meat was prohibited.[2]

The system was organized so that, as far as possible, the different needs of the different social groups were met. It based the rations to be allotted on research conducted in Great Britain, which found that 3,246 calories per day provided sufficient nourishment. The Swiss planners based the ration allocation on a slightly lower figure, 3,000 calories per day. In 1941 the figure was reduced to 2,400 calories, with the result that people grew visibly thinner. People doing particularly heavy work, such as lumbermen, steel workers, etc., were allotted supplementary rationing points. Children got special rations, to help meet their special needs. Sick people with medical prescriptions (which, of course, were not difficult to obtain) were given ration supplements for food they especially needed. Points could be exchanged for blue coupons that could be used to buy a meal in a restaurant. To check the effect the reduced rations had on the body, the staffs of a number of industrial plants were selected, and the workers and their families were given periodic medical checkups to find out whether they suffered from undernutrition or not.

There were special regulations for farmers and all other groups producing food of any kind that favored them as compared with the rest of the population. The simple reason for this positive discrimination was that they had to be motivated psychologically for the special effort they were being asked to make – and because strict controls were impossible anyway.

The whole system worked well, in spite of the insufficient total of calories the food authority was able to authorize for distribution. People understood the necessity for the short rations and as long as they were convinced that everybody was treated equally, nobody complained seriously. A fair deal is easily understood and accepted by the Swiss, but they would react violently against a real or a suspected injustice.

Even though people with a great deal of psychological insight presided over the rationing system, a psychological error was made in one special area. Foreign visitors to the federal capital, only too often officials instructed by their governments to tighten the blockade of Switzerland even more, were given the best the country still had to offer. It was reported that German, British, and American delegates judged the situation according to what they had eaten and drunk and concluded that the Swiss did not seem to lack anything!

Growing Food in the Backyard

It was evident that the accumulation of reserves and the rationing of the little the country had been producing could never solve the problem of survival in a world at war, a war that would probably be a long one. The country had to become self-sustaining for all those foodstuffs that possibly could be produced on the available land and under the existing climatic conditions. A great problem was the unfavorable balance between the different types of land: one-fourth arable, one-fourth pasture, one-fourth woods, and one-fourth unproductive glaciers, lakes, and rocks.

A committee of scientists was set up to develop plans for improving the nation's food balance. In November 1940, a national agricultural plan was published, largely inspired and conceived by Friedrich Traugott Wahlen, a professor at the Federal Technological Institution in Zurich; it soon became known as the "Wahlen Plan." The plan was immediately put into effect, and in the four years of its application, the cultivated surface was almost doubled. The acreage for growing potatoes was increased by 100 percent, for wheat by 46 percent, and for vegetables by 80 percent. This was achieved by drastically reducing the number of livestock and – at great expense of labor and money – by draining marshlands (480 square kilometers) and by cutting down forests (90 square kilometers).[3]

Manpower for reclaiming land and for cultivating it once it had become arable was of course scarce, since most of the time more than a hundred thousand men were under arms. Accordingly agriculture was mechanized at forced pace, not an easy task in a country with a highly fragmented terrain. Young people were assigned jobs in agiculture. Most of them, especially the youngest ones, accepted the unwelcome task good-humoredly, except for those students who belonged to organizations that thought it appropriate to protest against a national service they felt was beneath their dignity.

In these ways, agricultural production was expanded to the limit. The possibilities were not very great, however, because of the reduced work force, the small size of the country, and the high percentage of nonarable soil in the Alps and in the Jura. An additional resource was found. Under the Wahlen Plan, it was postulated that every square meter of usable land not otherwise used should be planted with vegetables by amateur gardeners. Soon 400,000 families were engaged, at every free hour, in practical gardening. Football fields, parks, roadsides, railroad embankments, and the lawn in the smallest garden became covered with potato blossoms, bean sticks, and tomato plants and after working hours would swarm with men, women, and children feeling they were doing patriotic work – and having fun. People were able to supplement the low ration of calories and at least could fill many a hungry stomach.

Industrial firms were obligated to buy or rent land for use by their employees. Some also provided tools, seed, and fertilizer, thus encouraging the good work. The result was not only an addition to the food supply, but also the birth of a warm relationship between workers of all grades – from vice president to apprentice – when they met at their allotments to compare the results of their toil. Growing food in the backyard and learning what it costs to cultivate the soil, albeit in a small and perhaps amateurish way, helped to prevent a conflict between the city dweller and the peasant – a conflict that could easily have flared up owing to the favored position of the farmer as far as food was concerned.

Many think that the Wahlen Plan made an important contribution to the healthy social climate that prevailed throughout the war years, in sharp contrast to the discontent and social tension during the final years of World War I, which culminated in a revolutionary movement in 1918.

Coal, Iron, Oil

For an industry producing mainly precision machinery, watches, high-quality textiles, and chemicals, all raw materials and all fuels had to be imported. The main purveyor always had been Germany. Before the war Switzerland imported 1.8 million tons of coal and 100,000 tons of iron a year from Germany; the figures went up during the war to 2 million tons of coal in 1941 and 200,000 tons of iron in 1942, but declined sharply thereafter to zero in 1945. Other traditional imports of coal, iron, and steel – 300,000 tons of coal a year from England plus steel from America and France – slowed to a mere trickle soon after the outbreak of the war.[4]

The machinery industry was by now engaged in a large armaments program. After years of trial and error, guns for the urgently needed modernization of the artillery were now manufactured by the state-owned ordnance factories. However, they had to rely heavily on deliveries of parts from private industry. For years, the world-famous Werkzeugmaschinenfabrik Oerlikon in Zurich, a private enterprise, had sent its antiaircraft guns and guns for equipping fighter planes to foreign countries but had been ignored by the Swiss army authorities who believed only in the products of their state-owned ordnance factories. Now in the Oerlikon works, guns ready for export were seized, and production and delivery to the Swiss army speeded up. Production of ammunition of all calibers and types was dramatically increased. Claims of all belligerents for war materials had to be met. Steel plate was needed for the rapidly expanding fortification program. Additional railroad freight cars soon would become a first priority.

A great effort was needed and achieved. By 1944 the national steel production had trebled. The main basis was the use of scrap iron. Scrap, hundreds of thousands of tons every year, had been a traditional export to Italy. These exports now were completely suppressed. Only the Vatican, enjoying a special relationship with Switzerland for which the pope's Swiss Guard was partly responsible, received 500 tons of scrap in 1943. The Vatican's blacksmiths and mechanics used it skillfully to repair elevators, heating plants, grilles, and crosses on churches.

Scrap iron was now transformed into steel in the existing Swiss steel mills, by the process of electroconversion. Since manganese, essential for the process, did not go through the Allied naval blockade, a search for this mineral in the Alps was pushed ahead. It was almost certain that along with the deposits of iron ore in the Gonzen Mountain, not far from the sources of the Rhine, there would be layers of manganese. Two tunnels were driven deep into the mountainside, and after nine months a lucky strike was made. In another nearby valley, at an altitude of 2,100 meters above sea level, an abandoned mine was known to exist. The army built a cable-car line to try to make reopening the mine feasible, but it was destroyed by avalanches. A second attempt, however, was successful, and the old mine yielded high-quality manganese, with the result that the total need, 24,000 tons, could be met out of national production.[5]

Along with the increasing production, all nonessential use of iron and steel was prohibited. In the official list of nonessentials were items such as signposts, fountains, bandstands, weathervanes, etc. The prohibitions, as the war economists knew, did not have much practical value, since the amount of iron saved was negligible, yet they were intended to be symbols, reminding people of the seriousness of the situation.

Nevertheless, steel still had to be obtained in great quantities from Germany, and steel was the main item in all trade negotiations with Berlin. It was fortunate for Switzerland that it had some small deposits of poor-quality iron ore – Gonzen in the Rhine valley and Fricktal near Basel – which could be delivered to Germany in exchange for steel. Iron ore was exported at a rate of 220,000 tons a year, a small quantity but considered so enormous by the Allies that at one moment they claimed it was helping the Germans win the war.

Coal could not be produced by any national effort. The few old coal mines in the Alps, which in World War I had produced some anthracite, were opened up again, but the yield of low-grade material was insignificant. The only way out was to induce Germany, in stubborn negotiations, to increase its exports to Switzerland.

On the other hand, it was imperative to save fuel wherever possible. Heating was the first victim; only 25 percent of the

amount of fuel previously used for heating was now allo-
cated. The Swiss spent a few cold winters indeed, but some
found it quite exhilarating and good for their health. Fortunately, the railroads were not the greedy consumers of coal
as in most countries. Switzerland had electrified its railroads
immediately after World War I because of its access to plen-
tiful hydroelectric power and because of its experience in the
years 1914–1919 when rail traffic had almost come to a standstill because of the lack of coal. By 1939, the rail network – 3,000 kilometers, about equal to that of the Netherlands – was 99 percent electrified, and electricity came from
local water power. Therefore, no rail-transport problem
arose, except for the scarcity of steel rails, sleepers, and
lubricants.

Diesel oil and gasoline were, of course, essential for the
operations of the army, in spite of its still relying heavily on
the use of horses. Liquid fuel was also essential for the
expanding mechanization of agriculture, and for the running
of the whole economy. Switzerland depended, and depends,
on imports for 100 percent of the oil it uses. The only sup-
pliers, after the sea lanes had been cut by the Allied blockade,
were Germany and Romania, and these imports became an
essential point in negotiations with the National Socialists.

On August 28, 1939, rationing of liquid fuels was immediately introduced. In 1940, fuel consumption by automobiles was reduced by 57 percent of the prewar amount; in
1944, by 94 percent. On April 22, 1941, practically all the
privately owned motor vehicles were immobilized. The only
exceptions made were for doctors and for those automobile
owners who could install contraptions that produced a kind
of gas out of wood or charcoal to run their engines. Yet,
because such machinery required the use of steel, even these
unsatisfactory contraptions were allowed only in special
cases where the owner could prove an urgent need and the
usefulness of his car or truck for the war effort.[6]

A chemical plant built during the years of economic crisis
in the thirties to utilize the waste wood of a poor mountain
area, the Grisons (Graubünden), now developed, with government aid, a motor fuel with an alcohol base that could be

used when mixed with real gasoline. Prompted by the air force, a chemical propellent for airplanes was also developed. Another firm produced a kind of motor fuel from coal and limestone. The quantities were small as far as total figures go, not quite 100,000 tons in the last two or three years of the war, but they were relatively important if one takes into account the desperate needs of the armed forces and the extreme scarcity of liquid fuels at the time.

Transport Problems

To the artificial obstacles of the two concentric circles of blockade and counterblockade that surrounded the alpine republic, the physical obstacle of a failing European transport system was added. In times of war, railroad cars, ships, and trucks become extremely rare items. Ports and warehouses become overcrowded or are destroyed. Marshaling yards are bombed, bridges are blown up, roads become unusable, and telephone links break down.

We have seen that Switzerland bought or chartered its own ships. On many occasions it had to send its own freight cars to foreign ports, to the Spanish border, or to Romania when there was news that some much-needed material had arrived. From 1941 to 1944 between 50,000 and 70,000 railroad freight cars were sent each year to Germany or the occupied territories to gather such goods.[7]

In 1940, on the basis of the War Trade Agreement, the British had given navicerts for 500,000 tons of various supplies from overseas. These supplies originally were loaded on chartered Greek ships, but after the Italian attack on Greece on October 28, 1940, Greek ships were not allowed in the Mediterranean. The 500,000 tons, therefore, were unloaded at the Atlantic ports of the Iberian peninsula, but the out-of-date Portuguese and Spanish railroads, the latter damaged in the Civil War, were not able to handle such quantities. In addition the goods would have had to be transshipped at the French-Spanish border from broad-gauged to standard-gauged railroad cars, an operation nobody was willing to perform. So Spanish, Portuguese, and Yugoslav tramp steamers were found to shuttle between the Iberian ports and Genoa, where the consignments could be handled. When Yugoslavia was overrun in April 1941 by the Germans, the Yugoslav ships became useless because, being enemy ships, the British navy would not allow them to enter an Italian port.[8]

On March 18, 1940, a commercial air link had been inaugurated by Swissair DC-3s between Locarno and Barcelona. There had been great hopes for this opening to the neutral outside world, but they were dashed when Italy entered the war on June 10 of the same year and the western Mediterranean became a war zone. The air traffic had to be stopped.

When navicerts for another 500,000 tons were issued by the Allies in December 1943, the question arose as to where such quantities of foodstuffs could be purchased. The North American market for the most needed articles, especially wheat, had been closed to neutrals, so the buyers had to turn to Central and South America. Yet in those ports the skippers would never be able to buy the fuel needed for the journey back. Swiss coaling stations, therefore, were set up on the Madeira and Cape Verde islands, the fuel being carried there by Swiss ships. Now the freighters could reach Central and South America and return with their cargoes.

To give just one example of the enormous complications involved in wartime shipping, let us look at the story of a small consignment of 6,000 tons of groundnuts bought in India in April 1940 – a small item but much needed. This example gives an idea of the kind of problems that occurred with practically every shipment. The groundnuts left an Indian port for Genoa on the British ship *Aenos*, under Captain Panaiotis Papadopoulos. Italy declared war on June 10, and the Mediterranean became a war zone. The *Aenos*, which had just sailed through the Suez Canal – as one of the last merchant ships to do so – was rerouted to Marseilles, where she arrived safely. The British blockade authorities refused permission to unload the cargo. Swiss representations in London were successful, the unloading began and 2,500 tons of the groundnuts were sent by rail to Switzerland. But the unloading took time and had not been completed when France sued for an armistice on June 17. British ships hurriedly had to leave all French ports.

The captain of the *Aenos* was instructed by the Royal Navy to enter Gibraltar, as it was feared that the cargo, being of British origin, might be seized by the Germans if it were in a Spanish port. In Gibraltar, the blockade authority inquired suspiciously what had become of the missing 2,500 tons (unloaded in Marseilles). Swiss steps to clarify the matter in London were successful, and permission to unload the cargo in Spain was now secured from the British. So the ship was allowed to sail to Cadiz. In Cadiz it turned out that Spain totally prohibited imports of groundnuts. After a month of waiting the Greek captain got bored and decided to leave the port. The Swiss obtained in Madrid an order for the captain to be stopped, by force, from leaving. On August 16, after special permission had been obtained from Madrid through diplomatic channels, the cargo was transferred to a warehouse in the port of Cadiz. In the meantime transport facilities were arranged with the Spanish and the French railroads. The freight train carrying the groundnuts was near Geneva, but still in France, when a bridge was blown up by partisans. So a fleet of trucks was sent into France to the stopped train, the groundnuts were transferred to the trucks, and on October 19, 1940, the final 3,500 tons were finally in the hands of the Swiss buyer.[9]

The difficulty of getting the much-needed products of the Swiss precision industry across the German counterblockade prompted London to suggest to Berne, in October 1940, that a direct, British commercial air link might be opened between Switzerland and England. In exchange, an easing of the blockade and additional navicerts were offered. The Swiss army held the view that no permits could be given for any foreign aircraft to land in Switzerland. At that time, the only commercial airport to speak of was at Zurich, located right in the middle of the largest military air base. The Federal Council therefore declined the offer. London insisted and proposed a commercial air link by Swissair via Spain and Portugal. This idea was taken up by Berne, but it met with open or veiled refusal in Madrid and Lisbon so the air link never materialized. It would, at any rate, have met with Berlin's opposition. Germany was most unlikely to have tolerated such a convenient channel right into the neutral country at the center of "Fortress Europe."

Toward the end of the war, when the French railway system was disorganized by Allied bombing and by raids by the resistance movements, it became necessary for the Swiss to send fleets of trucks to France to recover goods stranded somewhere on the way. Agreements had to be reached beforehand with the railway company, with the French government at Vichy, with the German military authorities, and with the various groups in the *maquis*. On August 8, 1944, the first of these convoys went as far as Lyons and Grenoble, often stopped on the way because of local fighting. It was actually not so much the lack of freighter tonnage on the high seas that created hazards for providing Switzerland with its most-needed imports, but rather the difficulty of arranging transport across a war-torn and increasingly disorganized and exhausted Europe.[10]

There was, of course, during the decisive years of the war, a major problem confronting shipping: the hazards created by the German submarine warfare. As long as the submarine war was successful, special measures had to be taken to permit a safe passage for the ships authorized to carry cargoes for Switzerland. A special bureau at the Swiss legation in Berlin was commissioned to assure the ships' security. By means of its own powerful radio station, the legation received the position and course of each ship and so was able to transmit this information to the German admiralty, together with a minute description and silhouette of the vessel. The admiralty then issued orders to the submarines to let these vessels pass safely. As a result not one single Swiss owned or chartered ship was torpedoed on the way to the ports open to Swiss shipping.

On the other hand the skippers had to follow the instructions of the German and Italian navies when approaching the Italian ports they were supposed to use. These instructions guided them through the minefields that obstructed the approaches. It is reported that the Allies were able to take aerial photographs of these ships while they negotiated the channels across the minefields and therefore knew what channels to use at the moment of the Allied landings in the Mediterranean in 1944.

Strange things could happen to neutral ships. In November 1942 two Swiss steamers in the Atlantic were nearing the Strait of Gibraltar when they suddenly found themselves in the middle of an armada of hundreds of ships heading toward the coast of Morocco. They crossed the stream of ships unmolested, and from the ships' signals Berne knew, long before the Germans had discovered it, that the Allies' landing in northern Africa was under way.

CHAPTER SIX

A Twofold Blockade

Two Concentric Rings

Seen from Switzerland's point of view, there were three distinct periods of the belligerents' economic warfare, during each of which the country's situation as a victim of the economic world war presented different specific aspects.

The first period was the time between the summer of 1939 and the summer of 1940, from the outbreak of hostilities until the entry of Italy into the war and the fall of France. During that time, exports as well as imports were, within certain limits, relatively free.

The second lasted four full years, from the signing of the armistice between France and Germany on June 22, 1940, to August 25, 1944, when the American armies reached the Swiss border and the encirclement by the Axis powers was broken. During this period, important modifications took place: in November 1942, when the Allies landed in North Africa and, as an answer, the Germans occupied the whole of France, and again on September 8, 1943, when Italy capitulated and, since it was not yet liberated by the Allies, was subjugated to the German terror regime. This four-year period was one of heavy pressures by both sides and of great privation.

The third period was the final stage of the struggle in Europe, ending on May 8, 1945, with the unconditional surrender of Germany. During that time the victorious powers increased their pressure on the neutrals, yet imports began to flow in more freely.

As we shall see, economic warfare evolved until two concentric rings surrounded Switzerland: the Allied sea blockade
and the German counterblockade. Both belligerents' measures originally were not aimed at the neutral country itself,
but at the enemy. Both sides recognized the right of existence
of neutral countries and actually did not try to destroy them
utterly but rather to harness them to their war effort. Yet to
make the economic measures against the opponent water-
tight, it was, of course, important to prevent any commodities sold to a neutral country from being reexported to
the enemy. This was the simplest, and one may say the most
legitimate, aspect of the economic warfare conducted by both
sides. The neutral did not suffer directly from it, except that a
neutral country had to give guarantees that reexport to the
seller's enemy was not envisaged and it had to comply with
complicated formalities.

Other problems arose when the belligerents addressed
their measures of economic warfare directly at the neutral
country. The Allies used every means at their disposal to prevent the Swiss from exporting war materials to Germany and
Italy and from giving the enemy financial help by extending
credit limits. On the other hand, the Allies insisted on getting
essential war materials from Switzerland. Concentrating on
the war effort, the Allies suppressed imports of merchandise
not essential for warfare, thus saving their foreign currency
for the essentials. Unfortunately, many of the traditional exports of Switzerland, one had to admit, were ill-adjusted to
war needs, items such as watches, shoes, embroideries, straw
hats, and so forth.

The Germans, for their part, made every effort to reduce
their traditional exports to the neutrals, especially where raw
materials such as coal, iron, and oil were concerned, since the
German war economy desperately needed these materials.
They insisted instead on obtaining more manufactured goods
of their choosing from Switzerland, mainly, of course, war
materials. By exercising economic pressure, they tried to
force the Swiss to reduce similar exports to the Allies and to
other neutral countries.

After Italy had joined the war on the German side and

France had been defeated, German and Italian soldiers appeared at all borders of Switzerland. The possession of French ports paved the way for extending the submarine warfare against the sea lanes. Berlin was now able to introduce, as an answer to the Allied blockade, its own counterblockade, and at times it was quite effective.

The German counterblockade was, as far as Switzerland was concerned, a sword with two cutting edges: the blockade on land and the threat of the submarine. From now on, nothing could be brought from the ports open to Switzerland – Genoa, Savona, Marseilles, Cadiz, Lisbon – across Italy or France unless Germany agreed. And nothing could be exported via these ports or on land across Europe without Berlin's consent. On the high seas the ships of Switzerland and other neutral countries carrying cargoes for Switzerland to the "Swiss" ports had to obtain the German navy's permission, protection, and guidance to pass safely through the submarine-infested areas.

Confronted with the opposed, yet like-minded interests of the belligerents, interests that were plainly understood in view of the desperate war effort everyone was engaged in, Switzerland had only one object in mind: to constantly try to break through the two blockade rings and obtain the imports necessary to feed its people and to run the industries that gave them work, provided the army with weapons and munitions, and produced salable items that could pay for the imports. This obvious confrontation of diverging or opposing interests opened up wide areas for pressures, threats, or blandishments and for complex negotiations at which, one may say, the Swiss soon became past masters.

Two concentric circles had closed around the small country in the center of Europe, and its economic survival now depended on how the interests of one of the blockading powers could be balanced against the interests of the other. In the course of this balancing act throughout the war years, Switzerland stuck to the principles set out in the 1907 Hague conventions 5 and 13 on the rights and duties of neutral powers in war, and especially to the principle of parity, that all belligerents have the right to equal treatment.

During those years, the Swiss, in their dealings with the surrounding world, often had to fight with their backs to the wall. They had little leeway for bargaining. Yet they knew also that the nations engaged in the struggle needed them. The existence of neutral territory in the middle of a continent at war was of a certain value for both the Allies and the Germans – even without the humanitarian and political services only a neutral could perform, of which mention will be made in a later chapter. Therefore, they knew that both belligerents had an interest – at least a marginal one – in avoiding steps that would jeopardize continued neutrality and make life impossible for the nation surviving in the eye of the hurricane. In desperate situations Switzerland's ultimate argument was based on its rights and duties as a neutral government, and on the principle *ultra posse nemo tenetur* ("nobody is obligated beyond his faculties").

Pressure by Germany

A few days after the outbreak of hostilities, trade negotiations with the Germans began. Berlin's object was to reduce the import of nonessentials from Switzerland and, in turn, to increase deliveries of products that would help the German war effort. Because of its shortage of foreign currency, Berlin also tried to obtain wide credit facilities. The talks led to a provisional agreement. New, more formal discussions began in Berlin on May 27, 1940, just as the German armies were sweeping across the Netherlands, Belgium, and France to their victory in the west. Now the National Socialists began violently to oppose the important Swiss exports of war materials to France and Great Britain.

The case of France was, of course, soon resolved by the armistice concluded with Hitler. Yet the problem of exports to Britain remained on the table. The Germans further insisted that war materials ordered earlier by Belgium, the Netherlands, and Denmark should now be surrendered to them. Berlin also asked for extensive new deliveries of war materials under the already existing loan policy to Germany, yet with much wider credit limits and on more favorable terms. It was suggested that Switzerland discontinue the War Trade Agreement of April 25, 1940, with the Allied powers, which strictly limited Swiss exports to Germany. To underline the seriousness of their requests, Berlin's negotiators threatened to cut off coal supplies completely, and Germany shortly made good on the threat on June 18.[1]

Now the Swiss were forced to make concessions, or else their whole industrial activity and their defense effort would come to a complete standstill. They promised Germany the manufacture of more parts for arms and munitions, the manufacture of more machine tools, the sale of aluminum already earmarked for export to Great Britain, and the sale of additional dairy products. The Allies were duly informed of these concessions, and their reaction was understandably sharp. As a consequence, the blockade authorities almost completely stopped the transit of any goods to Switzerland.

The trade agreement was concluded in Berlin on August 9, 1940. It conceded Germany considerable quantities of arms, ammunition, aluminum, and dairy products up to a credit limit of SwF140 million – soon to be raised step by step. In exchange, trains with supplies of coal and iron again began to roll. As a further point, the Swiss insisted upon their right to export war materials to the Allies in conformity with the principle of equal treatment of both belligerents. They also flatly refused to discontinue the War Trade Agreement concluded with London. This time the Germans had to yield. Together with the Italians they introduced a system similar to the British navicert. Goods of certain categories, about one-fourth of all Swiss exports, were allowed to cross the Swiss borders only if they had a special certificate issued by the German or Italian legations in Berne. For the remaining three-quarters, the Swiss undertook to make sure that not more than what had been usually exported before the war, the *courant normal*, would be sold. By this system a door was opened for certain exports through Italian and French ports, and also across Germany to Sweden and the Soviet Union. This door actually could be used.

Switzerland was even able to prompt Berlin, by expanding the credits conceded, to agree to so-called compensation deals. Compensation deals consisted of exports to Allied countries of articles they needed in warfare – via French and Italian ports to their final destinations. These articles, such as precision machinery, machine tools, machines for watch-making, transformers, electric motors, and watch movements, could be manufactured with components bought in Germany. This arrangement was made by the Germans in compensation for the right conceded by the Allies to the Swiss under the War Trade Agreement to manufacture articles for Germany from materials they had previously let through the naval blockade. The arrangement was of the greatest importance for the Swiss, since it permitted them (a) to keep their industry busy and (b) to pay the Germans for their iron and coal.

Throughout the war years, negotiations with Berlin went on. The pattern most of the time was the same: the Germans insisted on higher credit limits for their purchases in Switzerland and smaller deliveries of coal, steel, iron, oil, fertilizers, and gasoline, while the Swiss clamored for more coal, steel, iron, oil, fertilizers, and gasoline and for more transit permits (*Geleitschein*) for exports across the counterblockade to overseas countries and for imports across the submarine-infested oceans.

Sometimes curious and politically delicate negotiations became necessary. When Berlin, after having defeated France, asked the Swiss to hand over the arms, stores, and equipment of the French Forty-fifth Army Corps Daille, interned on June 19/20, 1940, Berne resisted the shameful request transmitted by a humiliated Pétain government at Vichy. The British wrote a threatening note saying: "If in existing circumstances the Federal Authorities should hand over these arms to the German Government which is still at war with His Majesty's Government in the United Kingdom and which would use them for the purpose of hostilities against His Majesty, this would involve a clear breach of the Federal Government's neutral obligations."[2] Under double pressure the Swiss tried to dissuade the Germans from insisting on the surrender and, after protracted bargaining, finally reached a compromise – one much criticized by an infuriated Swiss public, which was absolutely opposed to the surrender of all those arms to the hated Germans. In effect, the compromise meant that the Swiss bought, for a ridiculously high sum from the French government at Vichy, part of the impounded motor vehicles, most of which were fit only for scrap, and shipped the remaining trainloads of war materials to Germany. Four thousand horses had already been trotted back to France, where the farmers urgently needed them.

A new far-reaching trade agreement with Berlin was concluded on July 18, 1941, which raised the credit limit to no less than SwF850 million, interest free. The economic pressure was now at its height. Coal stocks in Switzerland were practically exhausted; lubricants were expected to last for only three weeks, after which time the whole industry and all transport threatened to grind to a halt. Under extreme pressure the Swiss now made a further concession that went very far indeed: at Germany's request they prohibited the use of letters or postal parcels for sending any articles abroad. This was a direct blow to the export of precision components to the United Kingdom.[3]

The new arrangement concluded with Berlin was greeted with wrath and moral indignation by the British, since it increased the deliveries of war materials to the Germans without widening the gaps in the German counterblockade for the benefit of the Allies and as due compensation to them. London called the agreement a "Swiss pact with Hitler."[4]

As time and the hostilities went on, more trade agreements were concluded, to be broken periodically by Berlin which would refuse to send coal, iron, and gasoline in the agreed quantities, whereupon the Swiss would hold back ball bearings, fuses, electric motors, timber, and dairy products — and new negotiations would become necessary.

The total hard-currency debt of Germany rose, by summer 1943, to SwF1.25 billion. The Swiss then insisted energetically that exports to Germany be drastically reduced, while maintaining all imports from Germany, and that the counterblockade be opened more widely. Berlin partly agreed, since the tide of war had now turned against Hitler. Exports to Germany in the second half of 1943 were reduced to about

Sw-F200 million; exports to the Allies, with German certificates allowing them to pass through the counterblockade, were increased to about SwF20 million.

The imbalance is striking. However, incredible efforts of will and courage were required of the negotiators to obtain even this unsatisfactory solution. The Germans had the colossal advantage of being in a position to cut at any moment the deliveries of coal, iron, and oil and to block all exports from Switzerland at its very border, leaving it cold and penniless. They could hint – which they rarely did – at the possibility of a military "solution." Actually, military threats were not used in the negotiations, but to the Swiss the presence of the far-superior German armies and the dangerous and criminal character of the German supreme commander always weighed heavily on their minds.

In defending its position, Berne could always remind the Germans of the possibility that the Allies, if deprived of all Swiss imports, would discontinue all their exports to Switzerland. This would naturally bring all Swiss industrial activity to a standstill and, consequently, all exports to Germany as well. And Berne could also hint about the possibility of interrupting all rail traffic across the Alps between the two Axis partners. Of this the Germans were more afraid than of the failure to receive manufactured products.

The last trade agreement with the National Socialist German Reich was concluded on February 28, 1945. It was practically meaningless, since German deliveries of coal and iron had diminished to a mere trickle of SwF10 million a month and the Swiss had stopped practically all their exports. The result was that in the last months of the struggle Switzerland again came near to the starvation point; the supply of cotton for the mills, for instance, was expected to last only another five days, and that of wool just a month.[5]

Throughout the years a few negotiators who had become specialists in dealing with the National Socialists performed a task far beyond their primary one of holding the balance between conflicting outside pressures. They became inured to stubbornly resisting unacceptable demands and were not afraid of antagonizing their opposite numbers when too hard pressed. Often the men at the negotiating "front" showed much more resolve than the government in Berne. It is known that the Germans were impressed by the attitude of these men and the fortitude they showed, especially when they felt that the Germans were trying to frighten them. From this experience Berlin drew the conclusion that its army would find it no easy task if it ventured to attack the fortress in the Alps.

However in the Swiss view, the threat of invasion always remained until the last months of hostilities. Only in 1945, if one excludes the remote possibility of some irrational, spiteful final onslaught by Hitler, did the threat of a military attack on Switzerland finally vanish.

Negotiations with the Allies

The Allied blockade took effect upon the declaration of war on September 3, 1939. The result was that no shipments destined for Switzerland, whether on Allied or neutral ships, were allowed into the ports earmarked for handling Swiss imports unless accompanied by the corresponding permit, termed "navicert." Navicerts could only be obtained on the basis of a special application made by the exporting firm. Most of the time, the port of arrival was Genoa, where up to 7,000 tons were unloaded daily until 1943 and carried thence by rail to Switzerland. The ports of Trieste and Marseilles also handled their share.

After protracted negotiations in London and Paris, the War Trade Agreement setting down rules for mutual trade between Switzerland, France, Great Britain, and also the other neutral countries under war conditions was signed on April 25, 1940. The Allied powers guaranteed, within certain limits, the transit across the sea blockade and their territory of Swiss overseas imports. They indicated the ports that could be used and the corresponding sea lanes, and they set down the rules for obtaining navicerts. The Swiss, on their side, pledged themselves to limit the export of certain articles to Germany to mutually agreed upon quantities. They guaranteed that goods acquired for exclusive use in Switzerland would not be reexported. Berne resisted the Allies' attempt to require undertakings signed by individual Swiss business firms promising nonexport; the Swiss government reserved for itself the exclusive right to control inside Switzerland the use made of imported commodities. Berne also obtained permission to sell to Germany manufactured products that used raw materials or components that had been allowed through the blockade. The total of these sales could not, however, exceed the total sold in 1937/38. This important concession was won with the argument that it was much better for the Allied cause that Switzerland pay for what it needed from Germany in manufactured goods rather than in hard currency.[6]

Matters took an abrupt turn with the defeat of France. The blockade was now tightened by the United Kingdom. The head of the Ministry of Economic Warfare, Hugh Dalton, and the parliamentary secretary of the ministry, Dingle Foot, now maintained that Switzerland, if too well provided for, might tempt its neighbors to military attack. They insisted that neutral countries should never be allowed to hold stocks for more than two months – a proposition that would have made life extremely difficult for the Swiss industry and population.

As a result of Swiss representations to London that it was in nobody's interest to push Switzerland into a position of exclusive dependence on Germany, navicerts were secured for a few hundred thousand tons of imports from overseas. At the same time, the system for obtaining navicerts was improved. Instead of individual applications by private firms for navicerts, the Swiss government was now authorized to submit a list of its general needs. On the basis of this list the blockade authority, if it agreed with it, would issue a block permission to give navicerts covering the quantity deemed legitimate. The system became known as the "inverted system."

The British, in the darkest year of 1941, felt that Berne made all the concessions to Germany and always rejected British demands. They became understandably bitter, and, on September 9, 1941, they prohibited the passage of all industrial raw materials through their blockade.

When the United States of America was catapulted into the

war by the Japanese attack on Pearl Harbor on December 7, 1941, the attitude of the Allied powers vis-à-vis the neutrals became one of greater determination. For America, which had been so stubbornly neutral, neutrality, once it was lost, became an anathema. Negotiations now became more complicated, since along with the Ministry of Economic Warfare in London one had to deal with the Office of Economic Warfare in Washington, and soon also with the Combined Food Board.

Now the colossally expanding American war industry joined the British industrial effort, and between them the two needed certain products from Switzerland more urgently than ever before. The list of items included machine tools, machinery for watchmaking, theodolites, chronographs (stopwatches), ball bearings, and, above all, jewel bearings – the manufacture of which at the time was practically a Swiss monopoly. Many microsized precision parts used in clockwork fuses could be made only by Swiss watchmakers.

Methods were devised to pass consignments of such articles through the German counterblockade beyond and above the quotas Berne had, in stubborn negotiations, been able to extract from the Germans as "compensation exports." One interesting case involved the chronographs. They were not included in the exports permitted by the Germans, since these stopwatches were extremely important to the Royal Air Force and the U.S. Army Air Forces in their bombing operations. Given that fairly large numbers of ordinary watches could be sent with Berlin's authorization, the ingenious watch manufacturers built stopwatch movements into ordinary watchcases, inoffensively showing two hands. Once through the blockade, the watches could be disassembled and transformed into the chronographs needed by the air forces.

A different situation, in which Switzerland only played the role of a transit station and a base of operations, arose over the need for diamond dies. Diamond dies, used in machine tools, were mainly produced by a very specialized industry scattered over small towns in France. Neither the French (Vichy) authorities nor the Germans would, of course, permit diamond dies to reach England. Consequently the raw diamonds and the necessary diamond dust were sent from England to Switzerland. From there, Swiss and French couriers carried the material to the manufacturers in France and returned the finished products to Switzerland. From there they passed clandestinely through France or Italy, finally to reach their destination in Britain. The operation could be conducted successfully because of the safe Swiss base located near the manufacturing centers.[7]

We have seen that in the summer of 1941 the Swiss prohibited the sending of small articles in letters or postal parcels to foreign countries. As a reply the British mounted a cloak-and-dagger operation under the code word "Viking." A none-too-scrupulous member of the diplomatic mission, John Lomax (now Sir John), set up a network of agents. They bought clandestinely the components of machinery needed – which, of course, required the full cooperation of the manufacturers. Other agents forwarded the materials in the diplomatic pouch, by special couriers, or by compliant neutrals – such as South American diplomats – to Spain and on to the United Kingdom. The Swiss civil air service to London or Lisbon, on which the British so much insisted, would, of course, have been the ideal solution for sending this priceless material to its destination.

The Swiss police and customs officers were, of course, fully aware of these clandestine goings-on, which were sometimes conducted in a rather naive way. But officers in both agencies gladly cooperated by closing both eyes. The same was true in the industrial end of the operation, where people were only too happy to cooperate with the Allies and to fool the Germans and their detested counterblockade.

However, the manifest sympathy these operations enjoyed wherever they were known – the circle had to be kept small to prevent German espionage agents from learning of it – still did not convince the Allies that the Swiss were not on the German side out of sheer greed. Up to the very end of the war one could hear that the only aim of the Swiss was to make huge profits and that they were actually responsible for the German counterblockade because they did not oppose it with enough determination. The Allies easily forgot that, when they forced Switzerland into a difficult corner by their blockade, they weakened its position in its negotiations with Germany. Lacking certain vital imports from overseas, Berne had to turn to Germany, and Germany then dictated its conditions before delivering the goods.

Nobody of course could see how much firmness and astuteness had been necessary to extract a concession from Berlin, and it was easy to forget that the Germans held the key to all imports into and all exports out of Switzerland. Any moment they could stop them dead at the very border, and even the mighty Allied powers could not prevent this until they had defeated the German war machine.

In their dealings with Switzerland during the years 1943 to 1945, the Allies concentrated more and more on one particular aspect: to reduce the sale of Swiss war materials to Germany. The federal government was severely attacked for the credits conceded to Berlin for such deliveries. Pressure was brought to bear on individual firms prominent in exporting to Germany by putting them on the blacklist. Blacklisting of course meant that all dealings with such a firm were considered as dealing with the enemy and were therefore prohibited, with all the ensuing sanctions.

The tension reached its culminating point in the summer of 1943. The Allies now presented the following demands: reduction of exports of war material; denial of further credits to Germany; stoppage of all rail traffic between Germany and Italy and vice versa. Collaterally, pressures on individual firms, spying by secret agents, and extortion of pledges not to deliver certain articles manufactured on the basis of German orders became standing practice. Finally, on November 4, 1943, the Federal Council put its foot down. It prohibited any single firm from having any individual dealings with foreign legations or their foreign trade officers and agents. As a sanction from their side, the Allies put such firms on the blacklist. In June, all imports across the Allied blockade had stopped. The same month several bombs—not very large ones—were dropped by British bombers on Zurich at a spot near the ball-bearing factories there. This was fully understood to be a final warning that all-out work for the German arsenals would no longer be tolerated.[8]

Fortunately, by December 1943 it was possible to conclude a new trade agreement. Switzerland now consented to reduce its exports to Germany in the first half of the coming year by SwF100 million. In exchange, the Swiss received navicerts for 350,000 tons of wheat, sugar, and edible fats. Berne could now more openly face the German displeasure over the reduction in the manufacture of arms and arms components. After the completion of the alpine redoubt by the Swiss army, and after the German defeats at Stalingrad and in northern Africa, the danger of a military attack seemed now rather remote.

In May 1944, the Allies demanded the complete cessation of exports of machine tools, ball bearings, and other war materials to Germany as well as drastic reductions in other items, such as dairy products. The Swiss did not agree to a total embargo, as suggested, but they conceded – delightedly, to tell the truth – substantial reductions. On October 1, 1944, the Federal Council issued a total prohibition of all exports of war materials. While the principle of parity was maintained – equal treatment of all belligerents – the prohibition actually affected only the Axis, since by now the Allies had become rather independent of Swiss products.

The Currie Mission

Gradually, the Allies' interest shifted from the war materials sold by Switzerland to Germany and the German counterblockade against Swiss war-material exports to the Allies to other matters concerned with the future: to financial matters such as the credits given to Germany, the enemy assets transferred to Switzerland, and the gold hoarded in the vaults of the Swiss National Bank. These all became the subject matter of new negotiations that began in February 1945.

The new round of negotiations with the Allies differed very much from the bargaining with the belligerents that had almost become routine in the course of the five war years. In the European theater the Allies were now nearing total victory. They actually could have dictated their conditions to

Switzerland; yet, true to their declared war aims, they preferred persuasion, coupled with the power of the economic factors, rather than coercion in their dealings with the neutrals.

The Allied leaders, Winston Churchill and Franklin Delano Roosevelt, knew how to distinguish between a neutral and an enemy country, a distinction that the Soviet ruler, Joseph Stalin, and also many subordinates of the three, sometimes found difficult to realize. The war was being fought on ideological terms, and it was indeed difficult for many not to fall victim to the oversimplification that those who did not fight against National Socialism actually were favoring its evil doctrines and criminal deeds; this was especially the case when the triumph over evil seemed so close.

In the earlier negotiations, the neutral country always had been confronted with the conflicting interests of two parties at war. The belligerents' reaction to every concession made by a Swiss delegation to one side had been a threat by the other side to apply sanctions. On the other hand the Swiss could use the argument that restrictions imposed by one side would weaken their position and their power to resist the other side's demands. Now, Germany had become practically powerless and was unable to exercise any significant pressure. The negative as well as the positive aspects of the dialectic had vanished.

Another new aspect was that now a joint delegation from the United States of America, the United Kingdom, and France arrived in Berne. The mission was headed by Lauchlin Currie, a special assistant to President Roosevelt, and included Dingle Foot, parliamentary secretary of the Ministry of Economic Warfare, and Paul-Henri Charguéraud, an official in de Gaulle's new administration. They spoke with one voice, yet the predominant role of the nation emerging from the conflict as a world power, the United States, was already clearly visible. The mere fact that the mission was called, from the beginning, the Currie Mission said enough.[9]

It was significant, however, that the chief American delegate was a low-ranking officer in the White House. This illustrated the fact that for the Roosevelt administration deal-

ings with Berne were only of marginal importance in view of
the momentous decisions on the future of the world that had
to be made at that instant. The Swiss did not realize this at the
time; for them it was most welcome and of great importance
to have, for the first time after several years, a direct and
serious contact with the United States. They were encouraged to give great significance to the opening of these talks by
a letter President Roosevelt had addressed, on January 19,
1945, to the president of the Swiss Confederation, Eduard
von Steiger.

The Swiss delegation was headed by Walter Stucki, a
former head of the government's Foreign Trade Division and
a former minister to France in Paris and Vichy. When the
Germans were driven out of Vichy in 1944, he had, by his
courage and skillful interventions, saved the city from
destruction. Whether his role in the new negotiations with
the Allies, including the French Gaullists, was made easier by
the fact that everybody knew the high esteem and friendship
bestowed on him by Marshal Pétain is an open question.[10]

February 12, 1945, the day the negotiations in Berne began,
was the day after the Yalta Conference had ended, the
very day the Americans left Yalta in a mood of supreme ex-
ultation, believing they had settled, with their trusted friend
Joseph Stalin, the problems of the world and would soon
achieve "peace for our time."

The main aim of the Allies now was to bring the war to an
end as soon as possible and to prevent the Axis powers,
which still appeared to them to be formidable, from again
becoming a threat to world peace. Since the coal shipments
from Germany to Italy via the Swiss railways were regarded
as an essential factor in the stubborn resistance the Germans
still offered to the Allied advance in the south, the first demand presented in Berne was to suspend that traffic completely. Secondly, the Swiss were asked to prevent the Axis
leaders from transferring important sums to Switzerland and
from hiding them in bank accounts and vaults for later use in
promoting their criminal designs. If such hoards already existed – and there was reason to think that they did – and if the
spoils of war were already hidden in Switzerland, they had to

be delivered to the victorious powers and/or to their rightful owners.[11]

On March 8, 1945, an agreement was concluded in the form of a simple exchange of letters. The Swiss had agreed to practically all the Allied requests. Yet, since most Allied demands affected earlier agreements made by Switzerland with the National Socialists, great care was taken not to appear to be breaking the old undertakings under pressure from the victorious powers. The Swiss were reluctant to seem to be using the victory of other people's arms in order to break faith with the vanquished. They could point instead to the fact that for some time now, Germany had not fulfilled its obligations and that therefore the Swiss were exonerated from fulfilling theirs.

In exchange for giving in to the Allies, the Swiss obtained the lifting of the sea blockade. From now on commodities were allowed to come in freely, with the exception of articles that were in short supply for the Allies themselves. And everything was subject to the limited transport facilities on land.[12]

The list of the Swiss concessions was a long one. Transit of coal and steel to Italy was completely suspended. Transit from Italy to Germany was drastically reduced, since it was assumed that it consisted chiefly of looted goods. Delivery of electricity to Germany was interrupted and the current diverted to France, insofar as France's widely destroyed network could accept it. Exports to Germany were reduced to practically nothing. Payments now offered in gold by Germany to reduce its existing debts to Switzerland had to be refused—a bitter pill for the government and many Swiss creditors. A credit of SwF250 million had to be granted to France, out of which repair work performed in Switzerland on French rolling stock and trucks could be paid for. All German assets in Switzerland had to be frozen and an inventory of all foreign holdings had to be drawn up. The embargo was to be lifted only after consultation with the Allies. The inventory was to be made by the Swiss themselves and all cooperation by foreign agencies was to be excluded. The result was to be communicated to the Allies. What was to become of assets so listed would be decided later.

More important perhaps than the freer flow of the neces-
sities of life that the Swiss had now obtained was the new
relationship of trust they had achieved with the Allies. This
was reflected in the terms of the communiqué issued to the
British and American press on the day the agreement was
signed. It said in its opening paragraph: "The Allied Governments fully understand Switzerland's unique position as a
neutral, a position which they have always respected."[13]
However, the problem of the German assets deposited in
Switzerland–gold and other assets–was still unsettled.

In notes dated August 3 and 4, 1945, the British, French,
and American governments informed the Federal Council of
a Potsdam Conference decision that they would claim ownership of and full control over all German assets in Switzerland.
The Swiss answered that in their view this decision was
devoid of any legal foundation. On October 30, 1945, the
Allied military high command enacted Order No. 5, according to which all German assets in neutral countries were to be
seized and transferred to the ownership of the Allied Control
Council. Berne was officially informed of Order No. 5 on
February 11, 1946, and the Swiss were invited to send a delegation to Washington to settle the liquidation and surrender
of the assets. Instead of helping the Germans prepare for a
new war, the assets would be used for reparations.

Berne sent a delegation, again headed by Walter Stucki.
The negotiations began in Washington on March 18, 1946.
After a series of proposals and counterproposals reminiscent
of dealings in an Oriental bazaar, an agreement was reached
that would have done honor to King Solomon: the Swiss undertook to liquidate the German assets and to share them
with the Allies fifty-fifty.

Gold presented a special and interesting problem. The
Allies had figured out that the Swiss possessed gold bullion
looted by the Germans worth one billion Swiss francs. In
addition it was known and recognized by the Swiss National
Bank that a part of the gold reserves of the Belgian National
Bank, entrusted in 1940 to France, had been surrendered to
Germany by the Vichy government under Laval and that a

part of that gold had been bought by the Swiss National Bank after it had been melted down in Germany. The Swiss offered to return gold worth SwF100 million to the Allies. The Allies, however, claimed SwF560 million, the amount they now considered to have been looted.

On May 25, 1946, an agreement was reached in Washington. The Swiss undertook to deliver 50 percent of the German assets seized in Switzerland to the Allies. They also undertook to compensate lawful German owners out of the remaining 50 percent and to pay them in German marks. Gold in the amount of SwF250 million was surrendered in New York to the Allies. All other claims to gold in Switzerland were excluded by this settlement. The United States of America agreed to unfreeze all Swiss assets that had been confiscated in that country. The Allies immediately suppressed all blacklists concerning Switzerland.[14]

Mutual trust and esteem was restored to a tolerable degree, and Berne could be content with the solution of this intricate problem—in spite of a great deal of criticism in the Swiss press made by people who had already forgotten that the Allies could have exercised overwhelming pressure and could have forced Switzerland, had they wished, to agree to a much more humiliating settlement.

CHAPTER SEVEN

Spies in the Fortress

International Espionage Center

It was well known to both the Department of Justice and Police and the general staff of the army that many foreign governments had centers of espionage in Switzerland, relics of World War I. Their task generally was to collect military, political, and technological information concerning neighboring countries. Switzerland was ideally suited for such activities because of its geographic location in the center of western Europe, its good railroad and postal communications systems, the continued flow of foreign visitors crossing its borders, its trilingual population, and in general because of the free and easy way of life and the relaxed attitude of the government. Absurd as it may seem, a measure forced upon Switzerland by Germany, for an altogether different purpose, helped the clandestine work of the agents assembled in Berne: the blackout ordered on November 6, 1940. Now it became an easy matter to stage rendezvous, visits, and secret transmissions of documents, sometimes in the romantic setting of the doubly dark arcades bordering the streets of the ancient city of Berne.

The command posts for espionage were generally located in the foreign legations in Berne and in some strategically well-placed consulates near the borders, such as those in Basel, Geneva, Lugano, St. Gallen, and Zurich. Protected by diplomatic status, the centers of these networks were practically immune from Swiss control and interference, and the authorities showed little interest in them since their activities generally were not directed against Switzerland, but rather against foreign nations.

The situation changed drastically when it became increasingly evident that Switzerland and its national defense preparations were also included in the list of "targets" of the secret services. The network centers were now watched more closely. Especially when agents who had been active in foreign countries turned up in Berne, it was easy to draw conclusions about the nature of their missions.

Military intelligence conducted in Switzerland against foreign countries was and is, of course, prohibited by law and punished under Art. 301 of the Criminal Code. When Swiss military counterespionage – which became quite proficient in the course of World War II in its efforts to protect the country – came across intelligence activities based in Switzerland but directed against other countries, it intervened. About 1,400 people were arrested because they were suspected of such crimes. About 40 were tried before civilian courts, of whom 245 were Swiss, 100 Germans, and the rest nationals of other countries.[1]

At that time the German legation was especially well equipped for espionage. No fewer than three parallel organizations gathered intelligence in Berne – the *Wehrmacht*, the Gestapo, and the NSDAP. They were also competing with each other in true German fashion and obstructed each other mutually. Among the spies working in Berne disguised as diplomatic or consular officers were high-ranking military officers, some of them on Admiral Canaris's staff. Especially when Hitler directed his war effort against Great Britain and other overseas countries after the defeat of France, specialists formerly active in Scandinavia and France turned up in Switzerland. However, as time went on, the work of this intricate setup concentrated more and more on Switzerland.

The American legation in Berne had been an important intelligence center during the last few months of World War I. Among its members Allen Dulles, a young diplomat, had received his first training at that time. When the United States of America was drawn into the Second World War at the end of 1941, the same Dulles arrived in Berne, practically by the last train on which an American diplomat could travel across the unoccupied zone of France. His particular mission, as was later discovered, was to watch and, if possible, to encourage resistance movements in Axis countries. He established close relations with the men of the 20th of July, helped them to communicate with each other and with the outside world, and in turn gathered from them intelligence on the situation in Germany and on military matters.[2]

The partisans in northern Italy and the French resistance members, who were of course infinitely more active than the Germans in their efforts against Hitler and his party, received decisive encouragement from secret agents connected with the American legation. The French *maquis* in the mountain areas just south of Lake Geneva communicated with their sources of supply of arms and food through the agents of the U.S. legation. The links with the partisans in northern Italy were especially close. These links also helped prisoners-of-war escape from Italy and Germany to Switzerland, and from there, they were helped across France to Spain or Portugal. The American consul general in Zurich, Sam Woods, was outstandingly effective in helping interned military personnel escape from Switzerland.

These links to resistance movements sometimes brought important information to Berne. One such report, obtained in Berlin through dissident officers, stated that the German agent "Cicero" had access to the safe of the British embassy in Ankara and regularly transmitted photographic films of the documents found there to the German embassy. Another scoop, probably obtained from the private intelligence service headed by the Social Democrat Otto Pünter, a Swiss, was the priceless information that Peenemünde, on the Baltic Sea, was the place where Hitler's secret weapons, the V-1 and V-2 missiles, were being developed and tested.

The Americans could transmit their information through channels available only to a country not at war, including the transatlantic telephone. The post office in Berne obligingly put a secret speech-scrambling device into the telephone line, to the great satisfaction of Allen Dulles.

The case of the Japanese legation and its intelligence work

was particularly interesting. Inside that legation two competing intelligence services were known to be working, one military, the other naval. Whereas the army group identified itself with the Japanese war party and was in close touch with the Germans, exchanging intelligence with them, the naval men, after the initial defeats in the Pacific Ocean, were striving for a separate peace with the United States. The latter also gave valuable information to the Swiss side. Neither group, however, was interested in Switzerland itself, but each used the diplomatic and other contacts that could so easily be established in Berne to overcome the isolation into which Japan was now plunged. At the news of Japan's surrender on August 14, 1945, the head of the army intelligence unit in the legation committed suicide. The men connected with the navy, on the other hand, enjoyed favorable treatment by the Americans.

One very effective espionage agency, working for a foreign country against other foreign countries during most of World War II, was located outside the diplomatic sphere and also outside Berne. It was the representative of Soviet military intelligence, which at that time could not rely on diplomatic cover since Berne had no diplomatic relations with Moscow. Using the cover of a Catholic publishing firm in Lucerne, Rudolf Roessler, an inconspicuous intellectual, carried on extensive intelligence activities. In criminal proceedings brought against him after the war, he succeeded in creating the belief that he was a kind of amateur agent, a Communist, serving various foreign countries and also Switzerland. What is more likely is that Roessler, a native of Bohemia, had been an officer in the Austro-Hungarian army during World War I, then a prisoner of war in Russian hands, and later recruited by Moscow's intelligence service.

"Lucy" (Roessler's code name) had valuable connections with former comrades, connections leading up to the highest ranks of the German high command. Roessler's information often proved to be accurate and of great importance. It was transmitted to Moscow by a Hungarian radio operator, Alex Radolfi, called Rado, who also ran a spy organization of his own. Rado had three clandestine radio transmitters operating, one in Lausanne and two in Geneva. Some think that Rado was a double agent. When they located the three transmitters in March 1943, the Swiss police closed them down and arrested the operators. Radolfi himself succeeded in hiding in Geneva in the house of a Communist. On May 19, 1944, Lucy was also arrested. These arrests by the federal police were not at all to the liking of Swiss military intelligence, since they closed a useful source of information.[3]

In his official report published at the end of the war, the chief of the general staff underlined the point that the several centers of espionage working for the Allies were almost exclusively involved with their enemies in the war and very little concerned with Swiss military secrets. It was a different story when it came to Swiss commercial and industrial secrets, which were high on the list of the British, French, and American services installed in Berne, since this information was directly concerned with the enforcement of the sea blockade imposed by the Allies.

Spying for Switzerland

Military intelligence had been neglected by the general staff in Berne during the period from 1918 to 1936 to a degree hard to believe. It can only be explained by the small size of this body and the general attitude toward its activities, which were not much more than administering and instructing the army. Intelligence was entrusted to one staff officer with a permanent assistant and occasionally an officer seconded for special research. As military tension grew in Europe, the service was gradually expanded; on September 1, 1939, the number of officers working in this branch amounted to ten, not counting the three military attachés stationed in Paris, Rome, and Berlin. At that time, the Anglo-Saxon countries were of no interest to the federal government in Berne, where hardly anybody could read English let alone speak it.

During the war the Swiss intelligence service numbered 120 members plus a still unknown number of secret agents. The whole was headed by Colonel (later Brigadier) Roger Masson. Its task obviously was to keep the Swiss high command informed about foreign armies, especially those of neighboring countries. The need to keep track of all military movements in a "critical zone" of three hundred kilometers around the country was especially stressed, and, as we now know, this whole area was covered in detail and with remarkable accuracy.

In the special case of any neutral country, one not involved in active warfare nor under assault, one topic dominates all others: Will there be an attack—and, if so, by whom and when? To answer these questions, the Swiss intelligence service had to develop extraordinary and subtle methods that almost permitted it to read the foreign leaders' minds. Spies had to be placed and infiltrated into their immediate surroundings. Obtaining information in the Axis countries was made easier by the existence of nonconformist groups, even in high places, which were able to watch the innermost circles around those who wielded power. A line designated by the code word "Viking," for instance, led right up into Hitler's headquarters and brought almost instantaneous, reliable information to the Swiss high command. Viking's operations centered on an officer in the headquarters' transmission center. Toward the end of the war this unique line was interrupted by a blunder made by the very head of Swiss espionage, Brigadier Masson.[4]

Before the war, a Swiss businessman and patriot, Hans Hausamann, had set up an information center. Its aim originally was to counter the Social Democrat party's activities directed at destroying the Swiss national defense structure and which, as it turned out, were responsible for so many shortcomings in the preparedness and armament of the army at the outbreak of the war. By the beginning of 1936, the Social Democrats began to revise their attitude of stubborn resistance to any kind of efficient national defense. They began to understand how much they needed armed protection for themselves, which only a strong army could provide, and they discovered their patriotic hearts.

Hausamann's agency now began to concentrate its efforts toward informing on the danger that a National Socialist Germany represented for its neighbors. Hausamann even established a fruitful cooperation with the Swiss Social Democrat party. His wide business connections in German industry permitted him to collect invaluable information about German intentions and military preparations. Gradually his organization developed into an intelligence unit that, at the time of mobilization in 1939, was integrated into the army's intelligence network as a special task force under the designation "Büro Ha." Its seat was moved from Teufen, a small town in the northeast corner of the country, to Lucerne, which now became the most important center for gathering intelligence.

A special branch office of the military intelligence was located in Lucerne and placed under the command of Captain Max Waibel – who was later on to become a corps commander. The mission of this unit, called N1, was to assemble all possible information concerning the Axis powers. Captain Waibel had been a student at the German war academy in Berlin up to the outbreak of World War II and was particularly well informed. What was more important, he understood the character of the German leaders and therefore of the German threat. The cooperation among Büro Ha, the army's N1, and other "private" spy organizations such as Roessler's Lucy bureau and Otto Pünter's private intelligence bureau, all located in Lucerne, became close and rewarding.

One may say that the Swiss actually knew the most secret activities in Germany and that their military countermeasures were a correct reflection of growing and diminishing threats. Inevitably in at least two cases, this intimate knowledge led to exaggerated fears. In these two cases the intelligence units transmitted serious warnings of imminent danger that at that moment did not exist, or at least certainly not to the degree reported.

On the days preceding May 15, 1940, concentrations of German troops north of the Rhine and transports of bridging material were ascertained and urgently reported. It later turned out that these movements had been part of a diversionary maneuver designed to make the Swiss believe in the imminence of an attack, and indirectly to prevent the French high command from moving forces placed near the Swiss border northward, where they were needed to strengthen the front under attack. A more careful analysis would have shown that the threatening signs were far too visible and that the Germans, had they really planned an attack, would have been more careful in keeping it secret.[5] Similarly, the false alarm that originated in Munich on March 19, 1943, has already been mentioned in Chapter 4.

Early in 1945 the intelligence service received information through its spies about a colossal German effort to build a mountain redoubt in the Bavarian and Austrian Alps, bordering on Switzerland, where Hitler was allegedly planning to make a last stand. This information was untrue; whether it was planted by the Germans or whether the plan actually existed but could not be implemented because of a lack of men and arms cannot be said with certainty.

The Germans always had the suspicion that Swiss military intelligence transmitted secrets its spies had gathered in the Axis countries to the Allies. They were encouraged to think so because in an unofficial and casual way Masson sometimes let them know secrets he had gathered from the Allies in exchange for valuable information from Germany. So the Germans made extraordinary efforts to find proof for their suspicion. Their belief also was founded on the view held in Berlin that General Guisan was a friend of the Allies and an enemy of the Axis. This he certainly was, but it did not prevent him from knowing perfectly well his duties as commander-in-chief of a neutral country. A similar informal exchange did not take place with the Allies, and from Masson's point of view it was not needed because Switzerland did not feel threatened from that side.

The relationship the Germans succeeded in fostering— through an intermediary, SS General Schellenberg—with Brigadier Masson and thus to Swiss military intelligence was especially designed to penetrate the secret of whether or not information was being given to the Allies. The relationship, at least in the German view, must have been a close one, since the Germans designated Masson and his closest assistants with code names such as "Senner 1," "Senner 2," etc.[6]

Masson's particular attitude, strange as it may seem, was part of a policy to appease the Germans, which he advocated. The Germans, however, never found what they were looking for, proof that they were fooled and that their suspicion was untrue. We know that personal relationships existed between foreign agents and Swiss intelligence officers whose duty it was to try to fish even in troubled muddy waters if the national interest required it. In doing so they evidently had to deliver, in exchange, bits and pieces of information that were of interest to their informers. However, any official or systematic transmission of information to foreign countries, which, unfortunately, was done in World War I – officially and on high levels – and which would have been treasonable, did not occur.

The colorful stories in the extensive literature devoted to Switzerland and its adventures in World War II, which go so far as to assert that intelligence from Swiss sources was instrumental in bringing about the Allies' victory, are simply products of the various writers' imaginations.

The General Among the Spooks

We have noted that the chief of the Swiss miltary intelligence service, Brigadier Roger Masson, did establish a personal contact across the border with SS General Walter Schellenberg. In Heinrich Himmler's *Sicherheitsdienst* (SD), "security service," Schellenberg directed espionage activities for a sector that included Switzerland. Masson was experienced enough to know that such a contact at the highest level would not help him gain information about Germany as military intelligence had to be gathered at much lower levels. But he gave credit to Schellenberg's assertion that he had access to the highest places and was frequently called to Hitler's headquarters. Masson hoped to use Schellenberg's supposed influence in high places for the benefit of Switzerland when it came to having to deal with difficult situations. And he hoped that he might learn from Schellenberg where the documents involving Switzerland, found in 1940 at La Charité-sur-Loire, had gone and be able to find a way of destroying them.

On September 8, 1942, Masson met Schellenberg on the German side of the Rhine, in Waldshut, and returned with surprising results. He had reached agreement on the return of one of his officers arrested in Germany and on the return to France, via Switzerland, of one of General de Gaulle's nieces and of the family of French General Henri Giraud. He had given practically nothing for these important concessions – if his violent verbal attack delivered against the Swiss press, which certainly was welcome to Schellenberg, is not considered a concession. From October 16 through 18 Masson met Schellenberg again, this time in Switzerland in a country place owned by one of Masson's officers, Captain Paul Meyer-Schwertenbach. At this second meeting Masson put the accent on dispelling the German distrust in Switzerland's neutrality. We do not know if he succeeded.

What did the German super spy expect to achieve by participating in these secret meetings? He certainly had two different things in mind. First, he wanted to find out whether the Swiss military intelligence cooperated, as the SS suspected, with the Allied espionage services. Secondly, he hoped to learn about the nonconformist officers in the inner circles of the German high command who were suspected of leaking information to Switzerland. An agreeable, good-looking person, well educated and witty, Schellenberg felt he was sure to win Masson's confidence and then to gather, from a slip of the tongue by his counterpart, the information he so badly wanted. These expectations, at least, can be discerned from the declarations Schellenberg made before the Nuremberg tribunal.

It is likely, but not proved, that Schellenberg had much more ambitious plans. Otherwise it would be difficult to explain the risks he took or the time he devoted to developing a connection with the Swiss. His dream probably was to open a communications channel to the Allies – via Allen Dulles in Switzerland – that would make possible negotiations for an arrangement that would align the Allied powers on the side of the Germans in the war against the Soviet Union. And finally, as almost every German does when he feels that the cause he is serving may be lost, he may have been looking around for "insurance" for after the war.

Encouraged by the meetings with Masson and the impression he was sure he had made on him, Schellenberg made a new and bold move, which met with Masson's full approval. He asked to meet General Guisan. The general accepted this rather extraordinary request, without consulting his government or his chief of the general staff. He stated his motives in his official report after the war in the following terms: "I did not want to let pass any occasion for confirming in our northern neighbor's mind the conviction which evidently was not strong at all that our army would fulfill its task under all circumstances and would fight against anybody attacking our neutrality."[7]

Guisan felt entitled to take the step without previous consultation since he knew that what he was going to say to his German guest was exactly what he had said repeatedly in public, and very recently in an interview for the Swedish press. This sounds convincing. But there is no doubt that the general had another motive that he did not talk about: his constant worry about the documents of La Charité that were in the German's hands. The lasting trauma of the 1939 secret agreements with France was instrumental in Guisan's agreeing to the meeting with the German super spy, which was, to say the least, most unusual.

Even more unusual were the place and form chosen for the meeting. It took place not far from Swiss army headquarters in a country inn, the Bären in Biglen, well known even in wartime for its opulent food. Schellenberg and his aide, SS officer Captain Hans Eggen, were brought to Biglen by the head of the Zurich municipal police and a crowd of plainclothesmen. General Guisan—flanked by Masson, Captain Meyer-Schwertenbach, and the Zurich police chief—sat down with Schellenberg and Captain Eggen around a table in a separate room of the inn. The girl servants moved in and out, the owner bid a friendly welcome, and the evening guests of the inn—excited that "the general" was there—tried to peep through the half-open door of the room. The talk during the hearty country meal was friendly and polite.

General Guisan raised his voice only once, when he explained to Schellenberg that Switzerland would fight against *any* attacker and that in case of a German attack the railroads across the Alps would be immediately destroyed.

After dinner the party signed the inn's golden book (the page was later torn out and disappeared), and Schellenberg and Eggen were driven to Berne. There they were put up in the most conspicuous place to be imagined, the Bellevue Palace Hotel, known to be the mecca of all spies in the country.

Not surprisingly, news of the meeting soon reached the federal government, a few members of Parliament, and the American and German legations. The Minister of Foreign Affairs and the Minister of Defense, Marcel Pilet-Golaz and Karl Kobelt, felt deeply hurt that they had not been consulted ahead of time. Some politicians tried to exaggerate the importance of the meeting and to inflate it into an *affaire* against the general. Guisan brushed all this aside in his quiet and unconcerned way by declaring that he had only done his duty by reasserting the well-known principles of Switzerland's policy of neutrality.

What was unusual, seen in the perspective of history, was the fact that the commander-in-chief sat down among the spies and that the meeting was staged in utter disregard of secrecy. Yet this disregard of secrecy, seen in today's perspective, certainly was shrewdly planned by the peasant Guisan.

Spying Against Switzerland

The rather casual view initially held by the Swiss about the intelligence work of foreign agents on their soil did not survive the late thirties. A new situation presented itself in 1938 when it became an undeniable fact that Germany had thrown a real network of espionage and subversion over Switzerland, similar to that discovered in unhappy Austria. The German agents were to provide all details concerning Swiss military defense. The political scene was also closely observed, with the aim of finding weak spots and ways in which to undermine Switzerland's will to resist foreign aggression. Plans for sabotage were prepared.

In the summer of 1938 the general staff alerted the police forces (which are decentralized and under the jurisdiction of the twenty-five cantonal governments) to the danger. At the same time it began to organize a military antiespionage agency called the SPAB (*Spionage-Abwehr*). It was typical of the naive approach of the time that it was thought that the task consisted of checking on foreign citizens residing near the border or close to other strategically important areas. Only gradually did it dawn on the antispy services that Swiss citizens could also be recruited to act for a foreign intelligence service. The idea is deep-rooted in the Swiss soul that a man who speaks the native dialect can do no wrong. For example, until the end of the war even the highest government officials thought that the German minister in Berne, who as head of the mission presided over all the machinations against Switzerland's safety, was a true friend—because he could express himself in the dialect of Basel. As we have seen, the Swiss members of the pro-German, pro–National Socialist parties and groups that sprouted after 1933 became the main reservoir for spies and traitors.

The intelligence service of the German *Wehrmacht* had a center in Stuttgart from which the espionage operations against Switzerland were directed. In the same city there was *Panoramaheim*, a place where Swiss traitors were received, housed, fed, and—in special instruction courses—trained for intelligence work, sabotage, and terrorism. Transmitting documents, writing with invisible ink, forging and using false identification documents, and making timebombs were important items in the curriculum.[8]

The places where instructions were given to spies and their intelligence reports were received were consulates and agencies near the borders. One of the most dangerous centers was one of the railroad stations in Basel, the Reichsbahnhof, located on Swiss territory but handling the traffic of the German railroads under German direction and enjoying a kind of extraterritorial status.

German military intelligence concentrated on four main aspects: fortifications, organization of the armed forces (in-

cluding the names and qualifications of the commanders),
new arms and ammunition, and the relationship of the Swiss
with the Allies. To obtain access to the secrets of the fortifications, agents with Minox cameras were sent to the areas concerned, and soldiers were bribed to indicate on maps the
exact locations of pillboxes, obstacles, and mined objects and
to draw plans of forts with their range of fire indicated.

To learn about organization and personnel, the traitors
stole orders and records and transmitted them to Stuttgart. By
listening to conversations in trains and inns – which in Switzerland are often conducted in the most careless way – they
collected information about the COs, their political views and
their private lives. The Germans were also extremely interested in modern weapons development and offered up to
SwF50,000 for an antitank gun and shell. Such weapons were
actually stolen by agents, but they never reached Germany
because the men were arrested at the right moment with the
stolen items.

The emphasis of espionage switched as the war developed.
In 1940 the Army Position and the three central fortresses
were in the foreground; after 1941 the National Redoubt, the
accesses to it, and the railroads became the espionage targets.

The Gestapo, the secret police of the SS, was interested
more in political information. General instructions issued to
Gestapo agents said, among other things, "Never forget that
we are interested in everything the enemies of Europe do,
say, and write; you are ordered to report on everything
related to the military and political warfare of the New
Europe against the Jewish democracies and Bolshevism. We
are extremely interested to learn about the cooperation of the
Swiss authorities with our enemies and their intelligence services."[9] Based on the work of its spies, the Gestapo prepared
lists of those Swiss – politicians, journalists, officers, businessmen, and intellectuals – to be liquidated at the moment
of a successful invasion. There were three categories: those to
be shot immediately, those to be taken to concentration
camps, and those to be closely watched.

Sabotage was planned against ordnance factories, air bases,
and especially against the prepared destruction of bridges. In

one case, which was discovered in June 1940, the cables for the ignition of mines placed under a bridge over the Rhine had been cut by saboteurs. On June 16, 1940, a group of nine saboteurs, seven Germans and two Swiss, set out from Berlin with orders to blow up the munitions factory at Altdorf and installations at the Payerne and Dübendorf air bases. Some of the men traveled on the same train but sat separately in different coaches. The ticket inspector noticed that some of his passengers had the same type of mountaineers' bag and wore the same kind of shoes. At the next stop he alerted the police who took those passengers off the train and arrested them. They all were carrying heavy loads of explosives in the rucksacks; they were sentenced to prison for life.[10]

In 1942 a sabotage plan against one of the factories producing synthetic motor fuel was discovered. In 1944 a group of frogmen under the command of the notorious German Colonel Skorzeny was spotted near the frontier, but still on German territory. They had orders to blow up bridges and power plants located on the Rhine, which forms one hundred kilometers of the border between Germany and Switzerland. Since at that time such objectives were heavily guarded on the Swiss side, the frogmen could not even begin their operations. Some of the German personnel in the power plants had already cooperated with the Swiss military guards in preventing sabotage attempts. The same Skorzeny force in southern Germany had orders to assassinate generals Eisenhower and de Lattre de Tassigny. The Swiss army learned of the plots in time to warn them both, so the attempts were thwarted.

Acts of terrorism in Switzerland were prepared in anticipation of an eventual German miltary attack. It was planned to set public buildings and newspaper offices on fire, to place time bombs in trains, and to explode charges at railroad stations and in the homes of officers and political leaders. The Germans thought the terrorist activities would produce panic and permit a military takeover without a real battle.

Looking back over Germany's feverish undercover activities against the neighboring neutral country, one is tempted to think that they were, in a strange way, partly responsible for the fact that Switzerland was not finally engulfed by the hurricane. The German leaders relied so heavily on their fifth column, in which they had invested so much, that they thought it would be possible to "conquer" Switzerland without a costly military attack. In any case they postponed that attack until it was too late.

Death to the Traitors

Defense against espionage and treason, which had been lacking in the opening phase of World War II, finally built up to a level of great efficiency. At the end of the war, one of the leading officers of the German intelligence service said: "After some initial weaknesses the Swiss counterespionage became by far the most effective one. The loss of agents reached the highest percentage in Switzerland. . . . There were times when almost all my agents had been caught or were at least forced to duck for cover."[11]

An analysis of the motives that induced Swiss citizens to commit treasonable acts shows the usual picture of pressures and blandishments by their German employers. Important positions in the New Europe were promised. Many a member of the pro–National Socialist movements in Switzerland acted true to political conviction. However, with one single exception, all the traitors caught had received or asked for payment. Some were cheated of their Judas silver by their employers in the course of a colossal game of corruption in which many German organizations, especially the Gestapo, were engaged.

After the surprise attacks on Denmark, Norway, Belgium, and the Netherlands and the onslaught against France, the full extent of the danger was realized and drastic measures were taken. The SPAB had already been functioning for over a year and had become very effective. The judiciary branch was also strengthened. By a decree of May 28, 1940, provisions were added to the military penal code to the effect that saboteurs of all kinds could be brought before a military court. Procedures were introduced by which counsel for the defense could not, as hitherto, use the knowledge gained in the course of the trial to surrender military secrets to the Germans. One lawyer who did do so was caught in the act and sentenced to ten years in prison.

The death penalty was introduced for the disclosure of military secrets and for military treason. The procedure was dramatically streamlined. In cases of imminent threat to national security, the military courts could, by unanimous vote, order the immediate execution of a person sentenced to death, ruling out any possibility of an appeal to a higher court or an appeal for reprieve. This summary procedure, however, never had to be applied.

The first death sentence was pronounced on October 9, 1942, in the case of an artillery soldier. He had been employed by an officer of the German consulate in St. Gallen to steal artillery shells, the design and material of which the Germans wanted to know. He was even expected to steal other newly developed weapons the size of a light cannon. In addition he was ordered to make sketches of important points of the Army Position. The man and his helpers were arrested on January 5, 1942, before he had been able to deliver anything. For all he had done or tried to do he had received a paltry SwF500.[12]

The total number of death sentences pronounced was thirty-three, of which fifteen were *in absentia*. Seventeen traitors were executed, of which fifteen were Swiss, one was French, and one a national of Liechtenstein. All but two appealed for leniency to Parliament, yet only one of them was pardoned by the deputies. The procedure then was dramatically fast: the minute the parliamentary vote had been taken and the appeal rejected, the army unit to which the prisoner had belonged was informed and ordered to execute him immediately. Among those shot were three officers (the highest ranking one a major), eleven NCOs, soldiers, or members of the auxiliary services, and three civilians. These executions had a visible deterrent effect. Along with the defeats of the German armies they helped to discourage the fifth column, which at one time posed a very real threat.

CHAPTER EIGHT

A Country's Privilege and Burden

Declaration of Neutrality

After Parliament had given the Federal Council full powers to maintain the security, independence, and neutrality of Switzerland and elected the commander-in-chief of the armed forces, the government issued a declaration of neutrality. It was dated August 31, 1939, and addressed to forty nations. The opening words stated:

> The international tension which has motivated the Swiss Confederation to take military measures, prompts it to declare anew its unshakable will not to depart in any way from the principles of neutrality which have for centuries inspired its policy and to which the Swiss people are deeply devoted, since they correspond to its aspirations, its domestic structures, and its attitude vis-à-vis other nations.[1]

All replies received in Berne were positive in the sense that the nations declared themselves determined to respect the Swiss neutrality in full. The British added a proviso to the effect that they would respect neutrality so long as Switzerland, for its part, would take all possible measures to defend and maintain a strict neutrality. Originally the British had made their agreement dependent on the condition that their opponents would also respect the neutrality. The Federal Council drew His Majesty's Government's attention to the fact that

such a condition would imply a belligerent's right to intervene militarily on Switzerland's territory without being asked
to do so, even on the simple suspicion that the enemy had invaded the neutral country. Berne insisted that Switzerland
was willing to defend its territory and neutrality on its own. A
belligerent could give aid only when expressly asked to do so.

The representative of the Italian Ministry of Foreign Affairs, upon reception of the declaration, remarked orally that
in wartime the Swiss press should show extreme moderation
in commenting and reporting on the international situation.
Switzerland's immediate answer was that such an extensive
interpretation of the concept of neutrality could not be admitted.

Thus, in the very first days of the struggle, two controversial aspects of neutral policy, as understood by Switzerland
on the one hand and the great powers on the other, had come
to the fore, aspects that in the course of events would occupy
Berne's attention time and again. First, Switzerland would oppose any attack on its territory and integrity with its own
forces and admit intervention by a foreign power in its favor
only when expressly requested. Second, Switzerland considered neutrality as a policy and an attitude of the government that excluded the military support of any of the nations
at war, pledging strict equal treatment of all of them but without recognizing any additional obligation.

A Neutral Press?

Among additional obligations that were to be repeatedly in-
voked in the course of the struggle, there figured conspicu-
ously the desire for restrictions to be imposed on the press.
The Swiss attitude, instead, was to the effect that an individual citizen had a moral right to take sides as long as he or she
did not engage in open acts in favor of one or another of the
belligerents. In principle, therefore, the press remained free
to report the facts and to express its opinion—but only in
principle. Since an overwhelming majority of the Swiss press
and radio had been, naturally, on the side of the Allied cause
from the very beginning of the war, they became the objects

of continual attacks and countless official representations from the Axis powers. In order to obviate such criticism and threats or, worse, a possible involvement in the war by military assault, which always appeared a possibility in view of the irritable and reckless characters of the two Axis dictators, the press and radio were subjected to government controls.[2]

Before the war, it was thought that in coming times of crisis the protection of military secrets would be the main problem. Consequently, it had been planned that such control of the media as there had to be would be entrusted to the military authorities. The government gave the necessary instructions to the army on September 8, 1939. The army issued guidelines to the press and the radio. It had put the task of restraining the media in the hands of officers who in civilian life were journalists, university professors, and people from similar walks of life. Their comprehension of the problem helped, and the system worked tolerably well. Censorship before publication was expressly excluded; only checks and eventual warnings after publication were admitted. However, when the danger of a German-Italian attack seemed imminent in 1940, countless instructions were issued to the press, visibly dictated by excessive fear and all directed at avoiding "provocation" of the Axis dictators.

It was unavoidable that a deep conflict would soon develop between the army censors and the media. The military controllers warned the press to be as restrained as possible, since they believed that it was in the country's best interest not to "provoke" by unfriendly words the dictators and the gangs surrounding them. The censors, as well as many soldiers in the ranks of the army, fell victim to the propaganda slogan, much used by the Axis press and Axis sympathizers in Switzerland, that, if it came to war, the press would be responsible because of its lack of moderation.

The media, in turn, were convinced that it was their patriotic duty to uphold the spirit of resistance by warning the people, by showing them the dangerous and reckless character of Fascism and National Socialism and of the nations dominated by them. The tension between the army and the media became gradually intolerable, and General Guisan asked the Federal Council to take this unwelcome burden off the shoulders of the army. He said that the military, if forced to continue the thankless task, could not help but introduce effective advance censorship. After stubborn refusals and the usual delays, the Federal Council, on January 1, 1942, finally transferred control of the press from the army to a civilian body under the Ministry of Justice and Police – where it was again a colonel, a university professor, who was put in charge.[3] Up to the very end of the war the struggle between censorship and the media continued, but at least and at last the army high command had been relieved of that particular responsibility.

It was and remained part and parcel of the neutral's burden to maintain the right of the citizen to be fully informed, to be free to express his preferences, and to condemn what was thought to be wrong. If a citizen was expected to fight, to sacrifice everything if it came to that, he had to be motivated. And motivation flows from knowing why. On the other hand, extreme expressions of public opinion and boundless partisanship manifested in the media could not be tolerated, since it could easily destroy the belligerents' trust in the willingness and determination of the government and the people to uphold a strict policy of neutrality – so proudly expressed in the declaration of August 1939.

Tragic Dilemma – The Refugees

If the record of Switzerland's World War II humanitarian activities outside its borders is a proud one, its handling of the problems of the displaced persons inside the country, or knocking at its door, can only be told with mixed feelings.[4]

After Hitler had come to power in Germany (in 1933), tens of thousands of his political opponents and Jews, rightly fearing persecution and worse, left their country. Many came to Switzerland, only to move on once they had found a place to go to and secured the necessary visas to go to their new homes. Some, however, chose Switzerland as their refuge and settled there. At the outbreak of World War II, 7,100 refugees happened to be in Switzerland, 5,000 of whom were

Jews planning to leave for countries overseas.[5]

The Federal Council and the bureaucracy were, at that moment, exclusively concerned with the immediate security of the country and held exaggerated views on the dangers involved by the presence of foreigners. Humanitarian considerations did not enter into their narrow-minded and fearful thinking. On September 5, 1939, it became compulsory for any person wishing to enter Switzerland to have a visa. On October 17 a decree was issued instructing the police to expel persons who had entered the country without the required visa; also it drew a distinction between "refugees" and "emigrés" – the latter to be under strict supervision and under obligation to leave the country as soon as possible. Accepting employment, whether paid or unpaid, or engaging in any professional activity was forbidden. Refugees and emigrés could be interned, and since there was no place prepared for their accommodation, many of them were simply put into prison.

The ban on work went to ridiculous extremes. One example was that of the famous Italian sculptor Marino Marini who, with his Swiss wife, fled before the Fascists to Switzerland. He was forbidden by the police to have any of his works cast in bronze and had to sell plaster casts clandestinely in order to make a living.

The brutality of the October decree and its application shocked the public, and it was strongly criticized in Parliament. Yet it was applied, and with even more zeal by the local authorities than by the federal police. This brutality contrasted sharply with the attitude of private citizens and especially of Jewish humanitarian organizations, which helped the refugees and emigrés survive precariously.

Since it became more and more unlikely that the emigrés would be able to continue their odysseys in the near future, special camps were set up in which able-bodied men and women were put to work. Tools and clothing they needed were sold to them for SwF65! In 1941 there were ten camps with about eight hundred inmates. These improvised camps were run mostly by army personnel. The army, of course, did not delegate its most able officers and NCOs to such an unwelcome task, with the result that often completely incapable people were entrusted with this difficult work. Unfortunate situations developed due to problems such as too heavy a work load (or, on the contrary, idleness), kosher food, or simply the despair of the quasi-prisoners, which stupid, or in some cases corrupt, camp commanders could not handle properly.

During the hostilities near the Swiss border in 1940 about 7,500 French civilians found a refuge in Switzerland and later returned to their homes. Several hundred Belgian and Dutch officers and soldiers trying to reach their countries' overseas possessions to continue the fight from there were accepted and interned in Switzerland until they found their way across unoccupied France to Spain. However, in the early phase of the war the problem remained under control, since the number of refugees was relatively small.

At the beginning of 1942 information about the mass assassination of Jews in the German concentration camps became fully confirmed. At the same time, mass arrests of Jews and their deportation to the occupied eastern European countries were reported from France, Belgium, and the Netherlands. The Vichy government declared 170,000 in France as "undesirable." Thousands of men, women, and children now began to penetrate into Switzerland and were admitted. It was now the turn of the army and governments of some border cantons to protest against the refugees' presence because they saw security risks everywhere. The federal government joined in this view because it was always exposed to pressures from Germany, which tried to make any escape of its victims to a free country impossible. The government also pointed to the fact that it was now practically impossible for any refugee to proceed to an overseas country. The way out was blocked, and anyway foreign countries were reluctant to open their doors. In the first half of 1942, for example, the United States granted thirty visas, Brazil thirty-one, and Argentina five.

A tragic up-and-down situation developed. At one time an order was given to Swiss frontier guards to admit political refugees. But were Jews "political" refugees? The government said no, but everybody knew that the Jews were in deadly danger, more so than the political enemies of the dictators.

The chief of the police department of the federal Ministry of Justice and Police, Dr. Heinrich Rothmund, always had before his eyes the threatening avalanche of 170,000 people earmarked for deportation waiting in France. He was informed of an actual concentration of hunted people in the wooded area north of the frontier around Pontarlier/Besancon. In order to dissuade them from trying to cross the border, he instructed his men to repel them at the frontier or, in the case of those found on Swiss soil, to escort them forcibly back into France. Incredible scenes developed. Some committed suicide in front of the Swiss frontier guards. Swiss officers refused to comply with the order to expel the wretched seekers of asylum. On August 7, 1942, the chief of the police department visited the frontier and remained there for several days. What he saw prompted him to lift the atrocious ban he had been responsible for himself.

On September 22, 1942, the lower chamber of Parliament, the National Council, debated the refugee problem. The official hardheartedness was attacked by speakers of all parties. The spokesman for the government tried to justify its attitude. He pointed to the danger that, along with the refugees, subversive agents might be smuggled into the country. He maintained that it was impossible to find work for the refugees and that, if admitted, a similar number of Swiss would lose their jobs. He repeated the well-known facts that it was impossible for emigrants to proceed to another country, that the security of the refugees also depended on the security of Switzerland as a whole, etc. He ended by admitting that humanitarian obligations were underlined in the very declaration of neutrality proclaimed in 1939 and by informing the deputies that in the night preceding the debate, 175 refugees had clandestinely crossed the border and had been given asylum.[6]

After the capitulation of the Italian army on September 8, 1943, a new wave of people in mortal danger reached the Swiss border. Since the fate of Jews at the hands of the Germans was well known, there could be no question of not admitting them. In September nearly 4,000 Italian civilians, many of them Jews, crossed the border along with more than

20,000 prisoners of war, mostly British, who had escaped from their camps when their guards laid down their arms and disappeared. The Italian civilians were placed in Switzerland in newly established camps. Many of them were from well-to-do families, difficult to satisfy and overly critical of the Swiss personnel.

Now, the jailers themselves, in Germany and Italy, began to fear for their lives. They came on the heels of their victims, seeking protection from the punishment awaiting them. On July 30, 1943, President Roosevelt issued an appeal to the neutrals not to give shelter to the leaders of the Axis powers or their criminal henchmen. The Swiss government replied that it would decide on the merits of the case, and without foreign admonitions as to who was entitled to asylum and who was not. They added that they had never heard of the term "war criminal" as a legal term. In September 1944 the American minister in Berne confirmed his president's message in more threatening terms, insisting that Switzerland was expected to not provide a haven for the Axis leaders.[7]

The Swiss meanwhile had prepared for the day when men like Himmler or Mussolini would turn up at a frontier post seeking admission. In an instruction issued by the police in July 1944 and in an army order by the general to all forces guarding the frontier, it was stated that "undeserving persons were not entitled to asylum." The order set down the rule not to admit "persons having assumed a hostile attitude toward Switzerland or committed acts in contradiction with the laws of war or who in their previous life have shown dispositions not consonant with legality and humanity."[8] Under this rule Mussolini's wife, Donna Rachele, was turned back at the border. With this exception only, nobody corresponding to this Swiss definition of a "war criminal" actually asked for admission. However, Marshal Pétain was honorably received at the Austrian border, allowed to drive across the country under escort, and handed over to the French police who arrested him. Mussolini was shot by partisans on April 28, 1945, on the shores of Lake Como while he was trying to escape, perhaps to Switzerland.

At the end of the dramatic year of 1944, the number of

refugees in the country amounted to 74,000, including interned military personnel and escaped prisoners of war. The number grew constantly. Camps were being prepared for 200,000. The official statement made at the beginning of the war five years earlier, that Switzerland could afford to receive only 7,000 refugees, was forgotten. In May 1945 the total was 115,000 refugees in camps: others, supported by humanitarian organizations, were in hotels, pensions, and private rooms or with relatives and friends. In the course of the war a total of 400,000 refugees and emigrants had found their way to and through Switzerland. One billion Swiss francs were spent on the humanitarian task that was often badly handled, it is true, but nevertheless saved many lives.

As we have seen, one of the main obstacles in the way of a more liberal and humane policy had been the ever-present fear that a Swiss worker might lose his or her job because a competing foreigner would take it. This fear obsessed the trade unions and the Social Democrats and was understandable in a way, since the recollection of the economic crisis and its concomitant unemployment was still fresh in everybody's mind. Yet, even people such as authors and artists and their professional organizations did not hide their animosity toward foreigners. This explains the ban already mentioned on engaging in any professional activity, paid or unpaid.

The situation of the 7,100 who had come and settled before the war was slightly better. A few thousand had become completely integrated into Swiss life. Among the Germans forced to emigrate after 1933 because of their political views or because of their Jewish ancestry, the proportion of intellectuals, writers, and actors was above average. Many were forced to continue their wanderings, but some found a new existence in Switzerland. For them the publisher Emil Oprecht, a Social Democrat and a courageous man who owned the Europa-Verlag in Zurich, played a great role as a friend and savior. Among his authors were names like Thomas and Heinrich Mann, Georg Kaiser, Arthur Koestler, Emil Ludwig, and Hermann Rauschning. Although hemmed in by book censorship and timidity and the incomprehension of certain officials, the list of books published in Switzerland in those years that upheld the cause of freedom and decency was impressive.[9]

Many German and Austrian actors, including many with outstanding names, found engagements with Swiss theaters. One of them, the old *Zürcher Schauspielhaus*, reached a high level of artistic achievement after 1933, thanks to emigré German playwrights, actors, and stage directors. After the annexation of Austria by the German Reich in 1938 and the fading of Vienna as a cultural center, the *Schauspielhaus* became the leading German-language stage of the world. Unlike the emigré theater troupes formed in Paris, London, or New York, which performed in non-German environments, the *Schauspielhaus* actors found in Zurich a large German-speaking, understanding, and sophisticated public, brought up in the tradition of German literature. Among the audiences, of course, one also found quite a few intellectuals on leave from their refugee camps.[10]

In such a setting, the evenings at that small theater often took on the character of shining manifestations of cultural freedom, human rights, and liberty—and were deeply appreciated as such. Naturally they were violently attacked by the pro-German, pro–National Socialist underground and sometimes had to perform under police protection. These refugees, many of whom remained after the war in the place where they had found a new home, helped keep up morale in the darkest times and thereby paid a hundredfold for the protection they were given by a free country.[11]

CHAPTER NINE

Stronghold of Humanity

The Red Cross

One of the many organizations that sprang into action at the outbreak of the war was the International Committee of the Red Cross (ICRC) in Geneva. The committee was and still is basically an association of private citizens, founded in the 1860s, but entrusted by governments with official missions. At the time of which we are writing these missions – helping in the protection of the rights of prisoners of war and of wounded and sick soldiers – were based on the two Geneva conventions signed on July 27, 1929, by dozens of governments. The conventions had been drafted by the ICRC in collaboration with many governments, signed at a diplomatic conference, and later ratified by a great number of states.[1]

A third convention concerning the protection of civilian populations in case of war had been elaborated and adopted by a Red Cross Conference held in Tokyo in 1934, but since a new diplomatic conference to translate it into international law was still pending, it had remained a mere draft – the "Tokyo project."

The belligerents were informed by letter, on the first day of the hostilities, that the Central Agency for Prisoners of War, as provided for in Art. 79 of the Geneva Convention Relating to the Treatment of Prisoners of War, was being set up. On September 14, 1939, it began to function in a makeshift building with fifty volunteer workers. By 1945 more than 2,500 people were employed by the central agency in twenty-seven offices scattered all over Switzerland.

The agency's tasks were to list all prisoners of war in a complete and up-to-date record and to transmit messages between them and their families. When the war was over, this register contained no fewer than 36 million cards, and 123 million inquiries concerning prisoners of war or missing soldiers and 23 million concerning civilians had been received and dealt with. The inquiries and correspondence of course went far beyond the officially registered soldiers. Information on missing persons had to be sought and transmitted to anxious families. The circumstances under which a person had disappeared, or had died, had to be established by finding witnesses or documents, often under extremely difficult conditions.

The efficiency and precision that became the trademark of the committee's work could never have been achieved without an incredibly fortunate combination of circumstances: A multinational corporation with its seat in Geneva was thrown out of business by the outbreak of the war. They used what were called at that time "statistical machines," which were now idle. The machines functioned with perforated cards, each carrying a great deal of information used in the corporation's bookkeeping. The corporation inquired whether the Red Cross might perhaps be interested in using such a card system and the machinery for its purposes. In order to adapt the machinery from the original task of handling the bookkeeping cards to the sorting out and retrieval of cards on which each prisoner was registered, the company asked the Geneva office of the manufacturer, International Business Machines, for guidance. They referred the matter to New York and on October 19, 1939, a cable signed by Thomas J. Watson, president of IBM, was received. It read: "Put machines at disposal. I recommend to offer rooms, cards and work free-of-charge in our offices Geneva." Thus began a most fruitful cooperation for the benefit of millions of human beings.[2]

Soon other tasks were added to the work of keeping track of and supplying information about prisoners of war and missing persons. The new tasks included visiting and inspecting prisoner-of-war camps; sending relief parcels to prisoners; submitting representations to governments in cases of infringement of the Geneva conventions or other irregularities; intervening on behalf of prisoners in the hands of governments that were not signatories of the Geneva conventions; transmitting messages between civilians and reuniting families; providing medical supplies; protecting persons not mentioned in the Geneva conventions, such as members of partisan groups and "irregular" forces; sending relief missions to concentration camps; and sending relief parcels to civilian prisoners.[3]

Many of these missions were undertaken spontaneously; they were not based on any international treaty or agreement but simply dictated by the urgent needs of human beings in desperate situations. Many such attempts were defeated by the inhumane attitudes of certain governments, but many more succeeded thanks to the moral stature the ICRC had attained and the prestige it had acquired by performing humanitarian services that only an organization based in Geneva could provide to all parties in the struggle. And by no means negligible was the fact, when it came to imposing the ICRC's will on reluctant governments, that all belligerents had the problem of their own prisoners and that they depended on the good offices of the Red Cross for their prisoners' comfort and survival. The only exception was presented by the Stalin regime, which regarded its own prisoners of war almost as traitors and criminals with no right to special protection.

Protecting Power

Under the Geneva conventions of 1929 a "protecting power" was assigned the task of assuring the implementation of the rules governing prisoners of war. The International Committee of the Red Cross assumed a similar mission, not because any assignment was conferred on it by international law, but simply because it obeyed "the call of duty." It derived the right to intervene from its mission to run the Central Agency for Prisoners and to transmit mail and relief parcels to the POWs. The fact was that delegates of protecting powers as well as those of the Red Cross visited the prisoner-of-war camps. Nobody knowing human nature will be surprised to learn that competition developed between these Good Samaritans who sometimes became bitter enemies, a situation that did not exactly further their cause.

This double involvement, however, also had its advantages. Supervision was intensified, and the governments could choose the organization they preferred. Germany, for instance, found it less harmful to its prestige to yield to demands made by the Red Cross, a private organization, than to those made by a protecting power, viz., a government.[4]

What in fact is a "protecting power"? When two nations sever their diplomatic relations and open hostilities, there are always problems remaining in each country that have to be solved through diplomatic channels. Each government therefore requests a nation not at war with their opponents to assume the mission of the protecting power, and entrusts its diplomats with the defense of certain interests on the enemy's territory. It was only too natural that in 1939 many of the governments drawn into the war chose Switzerland to protect their interests, since it seemed likely that it would remain neutral and thus able to perform the tasks of a protecting power until the end of the hostilities. The result was that Swiss diplomatic missions in 35 countries assumed at one time a total of 219 mandates to act as protecting power, an average of 6 per legation. Curiously enough, Switzerland frequently had to assume the simultaneous representation of countries at war with each other. For instance, Switzerland was the protecting power for the United States in Germany and for Germany in the United States.[5]

The task was not an easy one and certainly was not likely to win gratitude, since it implied the defense of the interests of a hated enemy vis-à-vis his opponent. It was easy for a superficial observer and an ignorant public to misunderstand the position of the protecting power as one of sympathizing with the enemy's cause. It was typical that the American press conducted a campaign against Switzerland, denigrating it as the agent of Germany. As a result of that campaign, the Federal Council, which did not have the courage to live with such hostility, laid down the mission of protecting power for Germany in the United States on May 8, 1945, the day of the German capitulation. It was not a courageous decision, and certainly not in the spirit of the humanitarian task previously undertaken with great success and still widely publicized.

One of the most successful and spectacular tasks of Switzerland as a protecting power was the exchange of interned civilians, including diplomatic personnel, and of sick and wounded prisoners of war. Early in 1942 no fewer than 900 Americans interned in Germany and Italy were exchanged for a similar number of Axis nationals interned in America. A total of 6,600 people were exchanged between the United States and Japan and 28,000 Italian women, children, and old men were repatriated from Ethiopia to Italy. Thousands of Jews, freed from the concentration camps, were brought to Switzerland. In August and September of 1944, 1,870 Jews were freed in Hungary and brought to safety in Switzerland. The price, in that case, was $1,000 per head paid to German jailers.

Switzerland always proposed and favored the exchange of sick and wounded prisoners of war and of medical personnel. These were delicate operations, requiring careful diplomatic preparation and a screening by expert medical commissions of those selected for the exchange. Success alternated with failure. In 1941 a Swiss hospital train with British soldiers reached Dieppe but had to return with its unhappy load to their German prisoner-of-war camps because at the last minute hatred and distrust made the already agreed upon exchange impossible. In 1943 and 1944, however, 10,000 wounded soldiers and 1,000 corpsmen were transferred to their homelands; in early 1945, another 7,000. The help of neutral Sweden and its sailors and ships was instrumental in most of these operations.

Most of these transactions involving the fate of thousands of human beings had to be conducted in the greatest of secrecy, and successes could not be published because the prestige of the nations at war would not tolerate any announcement of concessions made to the enemy, even when represented by a neutral. This explains why many of these actions were never made public and never brought credit to the protecting powers.

Another task was to provide "enemy aliens" and displaced persons in foreign countries with documents stating their identity and with visas permitting their emigration. Financial aid from relatives and friends of displaced persons could be transmitted only by the protecting power, although sometimes this was done by the Red Cross. The total sum of financial aid officially recorded in the course of the war amounted to more than SwF250 million.

As an example of the purely diplomatic services a protecting power could render, the transmission to Washington of the Japanese offer to capitulate in August 1945 must be mentioned. The exchange of dispatches between Tokyo and Washington was handled by the Swiss diplomatic service, but only in a technical way and without any material intervention.

The whole barbarity of World War II is reflected in the records of the activities of the protecting powers and their struggle against injustice and cruelty. The number of prisoners – prisoners of war, political prisoners, those persecuted because of their race, men and women in forced labor camps in Germany and the occupied countries – rose toward the end of the war to an estimated 20 million. Millions, whose lives were threatened, were protected, fed, and saved. It is estimated that humanitarian activities made possible by the existence of a neutral power in the center of war-torn Europe saved more lives than the total number of inhabitants of Switzerland, then 4.2 million.

Fighting Between the Fronts

The executive instruments of the International Committee of the Red Cross were its delegations, scattered all over the world. In 1939 their number was 3, in 1945 it had risen to 76. A total of 180 delegates, all Swiss nationals and many of them medical doctors, were working for the delegations, and each year twenty to thirty special missions set out from Geneva. The story of their often dangerous and adventurous interventions between the battlefronts is a fascinating story that would take volumes to relate.

One episode is typical of hundreds. In 1945 a delegate of the International Committee of the Red Cross was stationed in the infamous concentration camp of Mauthausen in upper Austria. The camp was guarded and defended by a battalion of the SS, five hundred men strong. When the American forces had taken the city of Linz and advanced eastward, the delegate was able to convince the commander of the camp not to sacrifice the lives of his troops and of the inmates but to surrender to the Americans. The *Kommandant* agreed on the condition that the Red Cross guarantee an orderly surrender without bloodshed. The Germans opened the gates and the barricades, and the delegate, waving the white flag with its red cross, drove toward the guns of the American tanks that were trained on him. The U.S. officer in command accepted the capitulation – also on one condition: that the Red Cross guarantee that no resistance would be met. How could he, powerless, "guarantee" anything? Only by exposing his person. The delegate now returned to the camp, followed at a distance by the tanks. As agreed with the SS, he found the tank obstacles removed. When the delegate waved his flag as a signal that the surrender was accepted, the German flag on the central mast of the camp was lowered and a white flag went up. The Americans entered the camp; the SS, who had laid down their arms, were lined up and guarded by the inmates, who greeted their rescuers with cheers.[6]

The number of relief parcels donated by governments and private humanitarian institutions to the Red Cross for distribution by that organization amounted, by the end of the war, to almost 100 million. The difficulties of packing up and sending these parcels were considerable. Sometimes the Allied sea blockade or the German counterblockade prevented the materials from arriving in Geneva or other centers of production and distribution. Quite often the routes to the camps were blocked. The governments holding prisoners sometimes were difficult to satisfy: Germany and Italy did not allow coffee to be included in the parcels (since it was powerful currency for bribing guards); the Italians allowed only khaki pullovers to be sent, the Germans on the other hand prohibited khaki pullovers or khaki shirts, and sometimes also those in gray; in Italy no boots, in Germany no shoes; no cigarette paper (good for sending secret messages); no cigarettes if the texts printed on the packages were deemed offensive. The parcels carried the name of the original donor and the Germans did not admit gifts from governments in exile not recognized by them, such as the governments of Belgium, the Netherlands, and the Free French government in London and Algiers.

Under the Geneva convention, visits to the prison camps were in principle entrusted to representatives of the protecting powers, but visits by Red Cross delegates developed naturally out of the work of registering prisoners of war and transmitting mail and relief parcels. These visits were in tandem with those of the protecting powers and were most welcome. The number of visits amounted to a mere 25 in 1939; by 1945 it had risen to 2,200 a year.

The nations that had not signed or ratified the Geneva conventions of 1929, among them the Soviet Union, Japan, and Finland, presented special and difficult problems. Urgent requests by the ICRC to apply the rules of the conventions at least *de facto* were partly successful in the case of Japan, but were rejected by the Soviet Union. Consequently, German prisoners of war in Russia were unprotected, and so, as a reprisal, were Russian prisoners in German hands.

Transmitting family messages—and transmitting the correspondence of prisoners—was, at the outset, not within the competence of the ICRC. Yet an urgent need for communicating across the front lines did exist, and only a strictly neutral organization could satisfy that need. The committee negotiated an agreement with the belligerents by which family messages of a maximum of twenty-five words were admitted. A special form (Form 61) was designed and adopted by 109 national Red Cross societies. The message could be written on it, sent to Geneva where it was checked for prohibited nonpersonal secret messages, and then transmitted to its destination. The number of such messages rose from a million in 1940 to 23 million per year by 1945. Every time a new country entered the war, an avalanche of messages arrived in Geneva, accompanied by a hundred thousand cables and letters written on unorthodox stationery.

When, with legalistic arguments, the Germans refused to recognize de Gaulle's Free French forces and later the French partisan organizations as regular armies and threatened not to treat those captured as prisoners of war, the terrible danger arose that the Free French would retaliate. The International Committee of the Red Cross succeeded, by urgent intervention, in obtaining for such prisoners the privileges applying to prisoners of war and thus prevented a massacre on both sides. A similar situation developed after the capitulation of the Italian army in 1943: the Germans disarmed it and threatened to deal with the soldiers as "interned military personnel." Their plan was, of course, to use the soldiers as forced laborers; they would not have enjoyed the protection accorded prisoners of war. Again the Red Cross was able to dissuade the Germans from carrying out the threat.

In the Greek Civil War, which broke out on December 2, 1944, the ICRC succeeded in persuading the warring parties to treat their prisoners as prisoners of war. It was even able to persuade the ELAS, the communist guerilla group, to free the hostages they had taken who had not yet been assassinated. ELAS also permitted the distribution of relief supplies such as warm clothing, blankets, and some food to the starving population.

The most dramatic situation for the International Committee of the Red Cross arose with the approaching defeat of Germany. Then all formal and legal obstacles that had stood in the way of its humanitarian activities began to crumble. Yet at the same time, the need for help increased a hundredfold.

From the outbreak of the hostilities, but especially from the beginning of 1942, when more and more information leaked to the outside world about the crimes committed in German concentration camps and about the mass deportation and assassination of Jews, the ICRC attempted to obtain access for its delegates to the camps in order to liberate the children, sick, and aged and to obtain permission to send relief parcels.

Needless to say, all requests met with a flat refusal as long as Hitler's armies seemed victorious. However in 1942, Professor Carl J. Burckhardt, who later became president of the ICRC, visited the German authorities in Berlin and succeeded in obtaining permission to send food parcels to certain camps, especially Theresienstadt where 40,000 Jews from many countries were imprisoned.

A difficulty arose because the Allied blockade authorities prohibited using food imported into Switzerland for parcels to feed the prisoners. Another problem was how to ascertain the names of prisoners to whom parcels could be addressed. It took real detective work to establish such lists of names. One method consisted of suggesting that once a parcel had reached a camp, the receipt be signed by several prisoners. Some receipts were returned bearing up to fifteen signatures. Geneva even succeeded in obtaining the names of prisoners who had been imprisoned for years without anybody knowing their names – the "NN-prisoners." In 1944 permission to send collective relief supplies was secured.[7]

Finally the War Refugee Relief Board set up by President Roosevelt in January 1944 engineered an opening in the sea blockade and sent relief parcels to Geneva, which then could be distributed by the Red Cross delegates. In March 1945 President Burckhardt was able to make a second visit to SS General Kaltenbrunner in Berlin, which resulted in important improvements. Swiss delegates were now allowed to enter the concentration camps, as long as they pledged to remain there until the war was over. These delegates distributed food parcels, prevented last-minute mass executions, and organized the peaceful surrender of the camps to the Allied forces – by persuading the German guards not to defend the camps as they had been ordered and had intended to do.

In addition, prisoners of war in Germany and the occupied countries now needed special protection. They had been forced to leave the relative security of their camps and were being marched toward the center of Germany. Fleets of trucks, painted white with the red cross, were sent to meet their columns. The French had provided the trucks, the Swiss had repaired and painted them, the Germans had assigned Canadian prisoners as drivers, the U.S. War Refugee Relief

Board donated the diesel oil and the food, and the Red Cross delegates directed the operations and saw to an orderly distribution of the parcels. On the return trip the empty trucks brought Jews liberated from the camps back to safety in Switzerland.

A Not-so-Humanitarian Mission

When Germany invaded the Soviet Union on June 22, 1941, an avalanche of propaganda was launched in the neutral countries. The war, a shameless war of conquest coupled with genocide, was advertised in Berlin as a crusade for Europe. It was inevitable that the pro-German circles, and the passionate anti-Communists, would eagerly espouse the slogans of this propaganda campaign. Some of them went so far as to propose sending a corps of volunteer soldiers to fight on the Germans' side against the Russians. All this was, of course, absurd, and few took such proposals seriously.

It was different when a plan was launched to send a medical mission to the eastern front. The authors of the idea, among them the Swiss minister in Berlin and Division Commander Eugen Bircher, who was in private life an excellent surgeon, had many good arguments to support the proposal. They said that it was the mission of the country of the Red Cross to give medical aid where it was most needed. They said that the Swiss military surgeons who lacked war experience would gain invaluable information and experience in the course of such a mission to the front. They added that the Germans, who were so bitter against the Swiss—even more so since German propaganda for their "crusade" against bolshevism was ridiculed in Switzerland—would be pleased by such a gesture, and appeased. The officers in the mission would be able to gather firsthand information about modern warfare.[8]

The opponents of the mission plan insisted that sending a medical team to only one party was unneutral, and would remain unneutral unless a team could be sent to the other side of the front lines. They distrusted Bircher, who had never hidden his pro-German feelings. They warned that such a gesture would have a negative effect in the Soviet Union and would hinder relations with that nation for many years after the war – in which the events proved them to be absolutely right. When General Guisan was informed of the plan, he immediately decreed that the army could not be involved in any way and that Bircher, if he wanted to go, would first have to resign his post as the commander of a division. Consequently, a private committee was founded on August 28, 1941. Among its members figured some of the country's distinguished citizens. The committee invited volunteers to participate in the mission, and those willing to go received a leave of absence from the army. Bircher, abetted by some members of the federal government, managed to keep his military position and to get a leave of absence instead of having to resign. The general was deeply angered and forced Bircher, at the end of the year 1941, to resign.

Since the Germans knew all about the plan and the BBC had reported it, there was no way back. The medical mission, all volunteers in fancy blue uniforms, left for Berlin on October 15, 1941, and reached Smolensk on October 24. The team consisted of thirty surgeons, thirty specialized nurses, and about the the same number of auxiliaries. The Swiss doctors and nurses soon endeared themselves to the wounded German soldiers. Conflicts arose, however, with Germany's higher military authorities when the Swiss could not resist the call of their humanitarian duty when it came to taking care of the Russian population and sometimes of a Russian prisoner.[9]

The first mission returned after three months. It was followed by three more, each of three months' duration. It is certain that a humanitarian task was fulfilled and that many lives, including lives of Russian peasants, were saved. Yet in view of the staggering amount of suffering caused by the German war machine, the effect certainly was marginal. On the other side, the medical information and experience the missions brought home were invaluable. Yet they also had witnessed German cruelty against civilians, prisoners, and Jews, and they returned with full confirmations of what was already known about the genocide that was occurring in Russia.

CHAPTER TEN

Negotiating Surrender in Italy

Italians Try to Save Their Country

Early in 1945 the war again crept toward the neutral island, this time from the south. The Allied armies had dislodged the Germans who had stubbornly held their Gothen Line in the Apennines. The fighting moved into the Po Valley, which is less a valley than a wide plain crossed by rivers and canals and is studded by some of Italy's most ancient, beautiful, and priceless cities.

Watching the Germans retreat, the Swiss high command became increasingly worried about the possibility that this area, linked to the Swiss Confederation by centuries of common history and common interests, might suffer heavy losses and damages in the fighting. The Swiss also possessed information, received through partisan channels, about German plans to follow a "scorched earth" policy on withdrawal from upper Italy. The partisans crossed freely into the Italian-speaking part of Switzerland, the Tessin (Ticino), where they brought information and received material support. They also reported on German plans to annihilate the partisan movement by the most reckless methods, similar to those perpetrated in eastern Europe.

On the other hand, it seemed likely that German Army Group C under Field Marshal Kesselring, still Germany's best combat force, might try to fight its way through Switzerland in an attempt to reach the planned mountain redoubt in the

Austrian and Bavarian Alps. Another possibility was that
Kesselring's twenty-five divisions would ask to be interned in
Switzerland, also a most unwelcome prospect. Yet the high
command of a neutral country could not undertake much to
prevent such developments, except to strengthen the border
defenses, which was done.

At that very moment, providence sent, on February 21,
1945, an Italian patriot, Baron Luigi Parrilli, on a secret mission to Zurich. Parrilli and his friends had been in touch with
the German SS in the hope of preventing the destruction of
northern Italy. They had figured out that they might engineer
a change of alliance in the sense that the German armies in
Italy would join the Allies and together they would oppose
the penetration of the Russians into southern Europe. With
such an idea in mind, in a dramatically confused situation,
and with some provisional agreement with the SS in his
pocket, Parrilli met a friend of his in Zurich, Dr. Max
Husman, who had many influential connections.

Max Husman owned a private school in Zurich, which he
had founded, and a boarding school on one of the nearby hills
in the lower Alps. For many years, in this rather plush estab-
lishment in the mountains, sons of well-to-do Italian families
had been educated. Husman, therefore, had been introduced
to the great houses of Italy. Early in 1940, seeing that the
Fascist government was leaning toward entering the war in
the wake of Germany, he saw the danger for Switzerland of
being encircled by the Axis powers. He also saw the danger
for Italy, about whose military preparedness he had no illu-
sions. So as a private citizen he made an attempt to change
the course of history on his own individual initiative.
Through his influential connections, he asked for an audience with Mussolini and was granted one. He told me
about the audience in his own picturesque way.

Mussolini listened attentively while Husman, as a Swiss
speaking with deep conviction on this matter, extolled the
virtues of neutrality and described the brillant future for Italy
if it too kept out of the military conflict. When he expressed
his conviction that Germany would lose the war in the long
run and drag Italy down with it to disaster, the dictator

became visibly impatient. Yet he asked questions and listened to the answers. At the end of the audience Mussolini rose, walked around his desk, and accompanied his visitor toward the door of his enormous *salone* in the Palazzo Venezia. Suddenly stopping, he turned to the visitor and, staring him straight in the face, made a balancing gesture with outstretched arms, palms turned upward. As he did so, he said in a grave voice, *"Guerra-pace—pace-guerra?"* ("War-peace—peace-war?"). Then Husman was dismissed.

A Swiss Mediator

Thus when Husman heard from his friend Parrilli about the plan to bring the German army in Italy over to the side of the Allies against the Russians, he exploded. He at once told Parrilli how completely unrealistic such a fantastic idea was. Nevertheless he sensed that the possibility of a separate capitulation of the army in Italy was in the air. He called Major Max Waibel, head of the N1 military intelligence office in Lucerne, whom he knew and trusted. The officer came to Zurich and met Parrilli. When he saw that there was a chance to avoid a disaster in northern Italy and that the ensuing military complications threatening Switzerland might be averted, he made a swift decision. Knowing that he must neither ask nor inform his superiors, who would have felt obliged to prevent any such—unneutral—intervention in the course of events, he acted on his own responsibility.[1]

Waibel informed Allen Dulles in Berne. For Dulles too, negotiation for a separate surrender was a hot potato. However, he encouraged the Swiss officer to go ahead on his own responsibility and promised to send an American representative if Waibel were able to organize, in Switzerland, a secret meeting with SS delegates. However the American representative would attend only to investigate the seriousness of the eventual proposals. Now Parrilli could return to Fasano, near Gardone on Lake Garda in Italy, where the German headquarters were. After a few days he sent word back to Waibel that he would smuggle two German emissaries over to Lugano, the Swiss city close to the southern border.

Husman, Waibel and a man from Dulles's staff met the two Germans on March 3, 1945. The Swiss informed the visitors that as far as they knew a capitulation could only be unconditional, that changing sides was out of the question and would never be encouraged by the Allied high command. Dulles's man hinted, however, that those who would help bring about an early unconditional surrender might, at the conclusion of the hostilities, certainly find it to their personal advantage. They were asked to send, if they could, a high-ranking officer to Switzerland if they seriously wished to negotiate the terms of surrender and, as earnest of their wish to lay down arms, to bring with them two Italian partisan leaders, specified by name, who had fallen into German hands. On March 5, 1945, a conference attended by, among others, Field Marshal Kesselring, SS General Karl Wolff, and German Ambassador Rudolf Rahn met somewhere near Salò, where Mussolini's government resided, and decided that Wolff should be delegated to negotiate with the Americans.[2]

On March 8 General Wolff presented himself at the Swiss border with the two completely bewildered partisan leaders. Husman met them and took them to Zurich. On the train he did a great deal of talking to try to condition Wolff for the coming meeting. Wolff met Dulles and finally promised to recommend unconditional surrender to Kesselring and to recommend that the planned scorched earth policy be canceled and the partisans spared, but only if they refrained from continuing hostilities against the Germans. In separate talks, Major Waibel received promises that the seaports of Genoa and Savona, so important to Switzerland, would not be blown up as planned and that the railway lines leading to the north would be spared. All seemed well and Wolff returned to Fasano.

Dulles informed his government of this exploratory meeting and that Wolff indeed seemed to be empowered to finalize the surrender. The Swiss mediator had suggested including a Soviet representative at the next meeting, but this was rejected by Washington. Field Mashal Sir Harold Alexander, the Allied high commander in Italy, now felt that he might risk making official contact with the Germans to accept a purely military surrender. He remained, however, deeply suspicious, and he wrote on March 11 to his government, "Two of the leading men are SS and Himmler men." On March 12 the Soviet government was informed in Moscow by the British of the talks with General Wolff.[3]

On March 15 two very high-ranking British and American officers arrived, in deepest secrecy, in Switzerland. Major Waibel and Dr. Husman had found an ideal meeting place at Ascona. It was a bungalow built over the water on the edge of Lake Maggiore (which I remember from happier summers – it still exists and now houses the bar of a grand hotel). The Allied officers were the British and the American chiefs-of-staff at Caserta, Lieutenant-General Sir Terence Airey and General Lyman Lemnitzer, and they duly met SS General Wolff and his advisers. They talked and reached agreement on the modalities of surrender, but not on its date. The capitulation was to be signed at Alexander's headquarters at Caserta.[4] The talks ended on March 19, and Wolff returned to Fasano. On March 21, the Russians were invited to send a representative to Caserta for the signing of the surrender.

Wrath in High Places

General Wolff's chief, Reichsführer SS Heinrich Himmler, had now learned of the decision made at Fasano. He immediately wanted to see Wolff; to make sure that he would obey his summons, he had his family arrested. Wolff was recalled to Berlin and interrogated by Hitler and Himmler. He succeeded in justifying his moves as a stratagem to separate the western Allies from the Soviets. Since a plan to lure the western powers away from the Russians was now Hitler's "ultimate weapon," Wolff got away with this explanation and was allowed to return to Italy. But information about the talks, suitably distorted, now miraculously turned up in the hands of the Soviet high command.

Field Marshal Kesselring was transferred to the western front and replaced in Italy by General Vietinghoff, making a delay inevitable. The latter did not know whether he should agree to Wolff's plan, and hesitated. Thus, no German plenipotentiaries turned up in Switzerland to be taken to Caserta. Everything threatened to go wrong. To the British invitation extended on March 21 in Moscow to send a representative to Caserta, Soviet Foreign Minister Molotov replied in insulting terms, stating among other things that "behind the back of the Soviet Union, which is bearing the brunt of the war with Germany, negotiations have been going on for two weeks in Berne between the representatives of the German military command on the one hand and representatives of the English and American commands on the other." Churchill decided not to reply to the letter, which he considered an insult to Russia's allies.[5]

In the meantime, the Zurich-Lucerne-Ascona talks had produced a serious crisis—the first major crisis of the Alliance. The Russians had by now constructed their own interpretation of the contacts—or was it perhaps an interpretation suggested to them by Himmler's agents? In a message cabled to President Roosevelt on April 5, 1945, Marshal Stalin said:

> My military colleagues, on the basis of data they have on hand, do not have any doubt that the negotiations have taken place, somewhere in Berne or some other place, and that they have ended in an agreement with the Germans, on the basis of which the German commander on the Western Front, Marshal Kesselring, has agreed to open the front and to permit the Anglo-American troops to advance to the east.

President Roosevelt was shocked and deeply hurt by these incredible allegations and the attitude adopted by his admired friend "Uncle Joe." He replied in the strongest terms, ending with the words, "I cannot avoid a feeling of bitter resentment towards your informers whoever they are, for such vile misrepresentations of my actions or those of my trusted subordinates."[6] Informed of this exchange, Churchill in turn sent a message to Stalin, on April 6, and associated himself fully with Roosevelt's final remark.

Thus, out of the modest attempt by two Swiss citizens to bring about an early surrender of German Army Group C in Italy, a major clash between the Allies had developed, including accusations that almost implied treasonable understandings with the enemy. Under these circumstances, Field Marshal Alexander ordered Allen Dulles to instruct Major Waibel in Lucerne to discontinue all his efforts.

The War Was Shortened

The deadlock lasted a month, during which time the struggle in Italy went on. Suddenly, on April 23, General Wolff turned up at the Swiss border at Chiasso, accompanied by high-ranking officers, and asked to be escorted to Major Waibel near Lucerne. He was taken immediately to Waibel's private house in Lucerne, and Allen Dulles was alerted and asked to come at once. He complied, but following his instructions, refused to see the German emissaries before he had been especially empowered to do so by Caserta and had telegraphed to Alexander's headquarters seeking new orders. Disappointed and furious, General Wolff wanted to leave, but Waibel managed to hold him back. Finally, a reply to Dulles's request arrived from Caserta. Field Marshal Alexander understood the absolute necessity of dealing with the matter in the presence of Soviet representatives rather than through Dulles in Switzerland. He therefore asked Waibel to bring the German plenipotentiaries together with the two Italian "hostages," Ferruccio Parri and "General Maurizio," to Naples. They flew there from a French airfield that adjoined Switzerland, not far from Geneva, on a military airplane Alexander had sent for them.

On April 29, 1945, the surrender of German Army Group C was signed in Caserta; it took effect on May 2, 1945. When Field Marshal Alexander put down his pen after signing, he turned to the war correspondents who were present and said, "This puts us practically in Berchtesgaden."

When the fighting in Italy stopped, Churchill announced it triumphantly in the House of Commons. He realized that the capitulation of the best German army still in a position to continue the fight, the first unconditional surrender in this final stage of the war, was the beginning of the end. So it proved to be. Six days later the remaining German armies capitulated; the struggle in Europe was over.

In northern Italy the British-American-French-Polish forces took over. A slaughter among the population and the partisans had been avoided; hundreds of cities and villages survived the war undamaged. Countless works of art were saved. Italy's industries remained intact and soon could join in the effort to reconstruct the war-torn country.

One may say that that German capitulation in Italy, almost a week before the unconditional surrender of the whole of the National Socialist empire, came perhaps too late to be really important. But it was at least of vital importance for millions of Italians and for one of the important centers of European civilization, since in a week's time untold atrocities could have been committed and countless cultural treasures could have been destroyed. We know today that the capitulation of Army Group C under Vietinghoff precipitated the disintegration of the remaining German armies. Without this precedent the war might have lasted another month, or even longer.

It is significant that the federal capital, Berne, was mentioned several times in the angry exchange between the Soviets and the western powers. Berne had always been watched suspiciously. Throughout the war there had been reports that the Swiss foreign minister, Marcel Pilet-Golaz, favored a separate peace between the western Allies and Germany and had been involved in steps pointing in that direction. The second part of these accusations is certainly not true, because Pilet-Golaz knew perfectly well the limits set on the foreign policy of a truly neutral state in such a situation. He knew that any attempt at mediation by a neutral government, favoring one side and splitting an alliance, would be both inadmissible and foolish. For this reason, it would be of little interest to comment on the countless allegations made during the war concerning Switzerland's alleged involvement in sounding out the possibilities of such a peace. Sweden, Spain, and others were far more involved in such proposals; the information concerning Switzerland does not stand up to the proof of hard facts. What is true, however, was that Pilet-Golaz personally wished for "peace at any price" and, being a talkative and imprudent man, made remarks to that effect, which could then be interpreted by his interlocutors in the way best suited to their purposes.[7]

To have brought about the early peace in Italy was not an achievement of the Swiss government. Neither the government nor General Guisan nor the military intelligence service (except Waibel) knew of the negotiations. Stalin's and Molotov's repeated allegations that negotiations had been taking place "in Berne" were, as we have seen, unfounded. Had the officials in Berne known anything, they would have prevented any further steps, knowing that such a mediation would have been considered a breach of a neutral's obligation not to favor one side in a war. But the neutral country of Switzerland, in the eye of the hurricane, was a platform for well-informed, well-meaning, and courageous citizens – and officers acting in an emergency as citizens – to do, on their own responsibility, what they thought was right and good for their country and for its neighbors.

CHAPTER ELEVEN

Deterrence Achieved

The Last Critical Days

From mid-September to mid-November 1944, the French First Army and the German Nineteenth Army confronted each other between the Vosges Mountains and the Swiss border. This border protruded far into the area that was to become the battlefield of one of the last decisive actions of the war. For the Swiss high command, how to prevent a penetration of the opposing forces into this northern projection of the national territory in the course of the battle became a serious preoccupation. The general was in a dilemma: on the one side there was the strategic imperative to remain strong in the main positions, including the Alps with their railroads; on the other side, the need to defend this narrow, yet very exposed area in the north. In his report published in 1946, the general wrote:

> In case we were attacked, even if it was only in this small projection of our territory, we had the duty to reply immediately with very effective measures. Our reaction at this very place was of great symbolic value for our own position vis-à-vis the world and for our own domestic situation. The slightest frontier incident could force us to take such countermeasures as would set fire to the powder keg and lead to far-reaching operations.[1]

Consequently, a whole division was thrown into the narrow strip of land. On November 16, the French army corps under General Marie Emile Antoine Béthouart attacked the

German front between Belfort and the Swiss border, intending to push as far as the western bank of the Rhine. Swiss territory was carefully respected. On a Sunday morning, the nineteenth of November, the American tanks and self-propelled guns with French crews turned around the northernmost point of Switzerland. General Guisan was on the spot, on that morning, to be with his forces in that most critical moment.

I watched as the last German trucks departed in an easterly direction. A group of German officers and soldiers had been left behind; they came across the border, at first refused to lay down their arms, and then surrendered to the Swiss soldiers. I watched as a French flag went up at the customshouse across the border, while shells still exploded over the roofs. Then I joined the general's party on the nearby hill. Lieutenant Colonel Barbey was there, the man who had been in charge, back in 1939/40, of organizing eventual cooperation with the French in case of a German attack in the very same area.[2] We talked and then the general turned around; on seeing me, he extended his hand to thank me for an article I had written on the occasion of his seventieth birthday on October 21. At that moment, an artillery shell fell not far from where we stood, but did not explode. Slowly, the battle moved north and east; far away, villages went up in flames, white smoke drifted from the fortress of Belfort. That evening, I described for the readers of the *Neue Zürcher Zeitung* the battle as we had seen, heard, and smelled it.

The fight on the border lasted, with moves and countermoves, until Christmas, when the Rundstedt offensive, far to the north in the Ardennes, began to dominate the situation for a week. Now, definitely, the critical days had passed. Or was quite a different menace looming in the near future?

After General Jean Joseph Marie de Lattre de Tassigny had crossed the Rhine with his First Army, he had led an armored spearhead along the northern bank of the river, chasing the Germans to the north instead of against Switzerland. This decision, which de Lattre later regretted, had been taken after a rather strange Swiss intervention. General Guisan, forgetting pride and dignity, had dispatched his son, a colonel in the cavalry, to de Lattre's headquarters to implore the French commander to push as fast as he could along the Swiss border to Austria. What did this mean? Only two possible explanations can be found for a move that so absolutely contradicted the general's record of courage and proud determination. The step was humiliating at a moment when Switzerland literally had been liberated from intolerable pressures, liberated by the sacrifice and the arms of other nations. And the step was unnecessary. Was it that the general's son, trying to give himself an importance he did not have, acted on his own or at least transgressed the instructions he had received? Or was Marshal Stalin on the general's mind? One likes to believe the request was made because the Swiss government and Guisan were afraid to see a Soviet army appear at its eastern border. And they had some good reasons to be afraid of the Soviets.[3]

By the beginning of May 1945, the French were well established in the Vorarlberg, Austria's western outpost, and militarily speaking the war was over for the Swiss. On May 8 and 9 the last shells fell on Swiss ground, the last few soldiers were wounded by shots fired at them by mistake from across the border. When the German army in Italy capitulated on April 29 and the unconditional surrender of the German Reich took effect on May 8, 1945, the Swiss could say that they had miraculously survived the five most dangerous years of their recent history. The strategy of deterrence had served them well.

The cost had been heavy, yet tolerable when compared with the sufferings and losses of the countries at war. Economically, Switzerland, far from making large profits in the war as an ill-informed public believed, had been forced to make considerable sacrifices. The cost of military deterrence was small when compared with the cost of actually fighting a war, but high when compared with the size of the Swiss economy. A look at the indebtedness of the federal government may serve as an illustration. Before the outbreak of the world crisis in 1935, the national debt had amounted to a mere SwF1.5 billion; it had doubled by 1940, and by the end of the war in 1945, it had reached SwF8.5 billion, which corresponded at that time to about $2 billion. It took thirty years to reduce it to a normal level; never again did it reach the low level of prewar times.

By the end of July 1945, the army was demobilized. August 20, 1945, became the day of the official end of the active service. It was celebrated in the federal capital, Berne, with thanksgiving and memorial services in the cathedral and in the largest Catholic church. In the afternoon of that day, all the army's banners were lined up in the square in front of the houses of Parliament. After short speeches by General Guisan and the president of the Swiss Confederation (then Eduard von Steiger), the banners were solemnly carried into the building.

Then General Guisan drove away. First, he went to meet the press and say good-bye. Minutes later he assembled, for the last time, the high-ranking officers (from colonels upward) around himself and outlined in a short speech his ideas for the future of the army in the postwar period.

Churchill and Stalin Have the Last Word

At the Moscow Conference with Churchill in October 1944, Marshal Joseph Stalin proposed an Allied operation across Switzerland in the hope of being able to turn around the Siegfried Line, which then seemed to be such a formidable obstacle to a British-American thrust to the east. He also planned to draw the Swiss army into the fight against the Germans. Churchill replied that such an operation would be counterproductive, since it would achieve the opposite of what was planned: it would add the strength of an intact Swiss army to the German forces. It would also be unnecessary, since the western Allies were sure to be able to force their way into the heart of Germany. This exchange finds its reflection in an instruction given by British Prime Minister Winston Churchill to Foreign Secretary Anthony Eden, dated December 3, 1944. In it Churchill refers to Stalin as "U.J." The instruction reads:

> I was astonished at U.J.'s savageness against (Switzerland), and, much though I respect that great and good man, I was entirely uninfluenced by his attitude. He called them "swine," and he does not use that sort of language without meaning it. I

am sure we ought to stand by Switzerland, and we ought to explain to U.J. why it is we do so.[4]

Stalin of course hated Switzerland because it was so fundamentally democratic and "capitalistic," because the Federal Council had opposed the admission of the Soviet Union to the League of Nations, and because he certainly had not forgotten the medical mission sent to the German army fighting against Russia. It was fortunate that Churchill opposed him. Yet it would have been difficult even for a Churchill to contradict a plan for an operation across Switzerland without the argument of an intact Swiss army.

Stalin's language at Moscow is not surprising when even in a democratic country such as the United States the opinion regarding the neutrals was absolutely negative. As Dean Acheson reported when describing the measures of economic warfare against the neutrals over which he presided as assistant secretary of state, "At home the public, almost to a man, regarded arrangements to supply the neutrals as traitorous connivance at treating with the enemy. Neutrals were judged to be enemy sympathizers."[5]

In the middle of such widespread attitudes, which, of course, were not shared everywhere and especially not in France, Winston Churchill declared in a note to Anthony Eden on December 3, 1944:

I put this down for record. Of all the neutrals Switzerland has the greatest right to distinction. She has been the sole international force linking the hideously sundered nations and ourselves. What does it matter whether she has been able to give us the commercial advantages we desire or has given too many to the Germans, to keep herself alive? She has been a democratic state, standing for freedom in self-defence among her mountains, and in thought, in spite of race, largely on our side.[6]

Notes

General

1. *The government of Switzerland.* The 1848 Constitution creating the federal state was deeply influenced by the American Constitution of 1787. The Swiss Confederation consists of the cantons, which correspond to the states of the United States. The Parliament is divided into two houses: the National Council (corresponding more or less to the U.S. House of Representatives) and the Council of States (corresponding, *cum grano salis*, to the U.S. Senate). Every four years, they jointly elect the executive, which is a seven-member committee called the Federal Council. Each councillor is a cabinet minister, the head of one of the seven ministries (departments) into which the federal administration is divided: Interior (cultural affairs), Foreign Affairs, Finances, Economics, Defense, Justice and Police, Post and Railroads (today Energy and Transports).

There is no prime minister, no head of government. The Federal Council is a collegium, with a president who changes each year and who has no greater powers than any of his colleagues in the executive. During the year of his presidency, he remains the head of his particular ministry, but he carries the title of president of the confederation. He actually is not the head of state. Also, the council, while composed of representatives of four parties, is no ordinary coalition government for the councillors are supposed to cease to behave as party men on assuming their high office.

Once elected by the federal Parliament, ministers as a rule are reelected should they wish to remain in office; occasionally, however, members of the government have been persuaded not to seek reelection. Cabinet crises and votes of censure or nonconfidence are unknown, and neither a parliamentary vote nor a referendum will cause the governmênt to resign.

2. *Translations*. In the text, German and French quotations have been translated into English by the author.

Preface

1. Michel de Montaigne, *Essais* (Paris, 1823), bk. 3, chap. 8, p. 460.

2. See the *Selected Bibliography*, which lists a number of titles that are not mentioned in the notes but are part of the background of the present work.

Chapter 1. Electing the General

1. Fritz Ernst, *Generäle* (Zurich, 1942), 117, 153.

2. See Notes, General, for information on the government of Switzerland.

3. Edgar Bonjour, *Geschichte der schweizerischen Neutralität* (Basel, 1970), 3:283.

4. Klaus Urner, "Der Schweizer Hitler-Attentäter Maurice Bavaud," *Neue Zürcher Zeitung*, July 1978, Nos. 150, 153, 155 (Zurich, 1978).

5. Bonjour, *Geschichte*, 3:295.

6. Ibid., 3:89 ff.

7. Ibid., 4:393.

8. Oscar A. Germann, *Erinnerungen* (Berne, 1978).

9. Bonjour, *Geschichte*, 4:70.

Chapter 2. Secret Agreements for Survival

1. Edgar Bonjour, *Geschichte der schweizerischen Neutralität* (Basel, 1970), 5:33.

2. Maxime Weygand, *Mémoires: Idéal vécu* (Paris, 1953), 385.

3. René-Henri Wüst, *Alerte en pays neutre: La Suisse en 1940* (Lausanne, 1966), 72.

4. Bernard Barbey, *Aller et retour: Mon journal pendant et après la "drôle de guerre" 1939–1940* (Neuchâtel, 1967), 22.

5. Oscar A. Germann, *Erinnerungen* (Berne, 1978), 65.

6. Barbey, *Aller et retour*, 174.

7. Wüst, *Alerte en pays neutre*, 45.

8. Bonjour, *Geschichte*, 5:13 ff.

9. Hans Rudolf Kurz, *Die Schweiz in der Planung der kriegführenden Mächte während des zweiten Weltkrieges* (Biel, 1957), 23.

Chapter 3. The Hurricane Breaks Loose

1. Hans Rudolf Kurz, *Die Schweiz in der Planung der kriegführenden Mächte während des zweiten Weltkrieges* (Biel, 1957), 17.
2. Vincent J. Esposito, *The West Point Atlas of American Wars 1900–1953* (New York, 1959), 2:13.
3. René-Henri Wüst, *Alerte en pays neutre: La Suisse en 1940* (Lausanne, 1966), 90.
4. Edgar Bonjour, *Geschichte der schweizerischen Neutralität* (Basel, 1970), 4:81.
5. General Henri Guisan, *Bericht an die Bundesversammlung über den Aktivdienst 1939–1945* (Berne, 1946), Annex II.
6. Bonjour, *Geschichte*, 4:97.
7. Ibid., 5:123, 124.
8. Ibid., 5:131.
9. Ibid., 5:132, n. 55.
10. Ibid., 4:113.
11. Ibid., 4:119.
12. Erwin Bucher, "Der grosse Schock des Sommers 1940," *Neue Zürcher Zeitung*, May 1979, Nos. 100, 113, 119 (Zurich 1979).
13. Klaus Urner, "Neue Bewertungskriterien im Fall Pilet-Golaz," *Neue Zürcher Zeitung*, January 1978, No. 20 (Zurich, 1978).
14. Bonjour, *Geschichte*, 4:189.
15. Wüst, *Alerte en pays neutre*, 106.
16. Bonjour, *Geschichte*, 4:360.
17. Gerhart Waeger, *Die Sündenböcke der Schweiz: Die Zweihundert im Urteil der geschichtlichen Dokumente 1940–1946* (Olten, 1971), 148.

Chapter 4. Fortress Switzerland

1. Bernard Barbey, *Aller et retour: Mon journal pendant et après la "drôle de guerre" 1939–1940* (Neuchâtel, 1967), 132.
2. General Henri Guisan, *Bericht an die Bundesversammlung über den Aktivdienst 1939–1945* (Berne, 1946), 33.
3. Oscar A. Germann, *Erinnerungen* (Berne, 1978), 69.
4. Bernard Barbey, *P. C. du Général: Journal du chef de l'état major particulier du Général Guisan 1940–1945* (Neuchâtel, 1948), 24.

5. Hans Rudolf Kurz, *Die Schweiz in der Planung der kriegführenden Mächte während des zweiten Weltkrieges* (Biel, 1957), 26.

6. Thucydides, *Thucydidis de bello peloponnesiaco libri octo* (Biponti, 1788), bk. 1, 143 ("suaderem, ut vos ipsi ex urbe exeuntes has res vastaretis et Peloponnesiis demonstraretis, vos harum rerum causa imperata non facturos").

7. Guisan, *Bericht an die Bundesversammlung*, 37.

8. Peter Dürrenmatt, *Schweizer Geschichte* (Zurich, 1976), 2:911.

9. Barbey, *P.C. du Général*, 30.

10. *Neue Zürcher Zeitung*, July 29, 1940.

11. Edgar Bonjour, *Geschichte der schweizerischen Neutralität* (Basel, 1970), 4:379.

12. Ibid., 4:241.

13. Ibid., 4:226.

14. Jakob Huber, *Bericht des Chefs des Generalstabs an den Oberbefehlshaber der Armee über den Aktivdienst 1939–1945* (Berne, 1946), 41.

15. Barbey, *P. C. du Général*, 128.

16. Kurz, *Die Schweiz in der Planung*, 28.

17. Ibid., 49.

18. Ibid., 39.

19. Alfred Ernst, *Die Konzeption der schweizerischen Landesverteidigung 1815 bis 1966* (Frauenfeld, 1971), 69, n. 32.

20. Bonjour, *Geschichte*, 6:271.

21. Dean Acheson, *Present at the Creation: My Years in the State Department* (New York, 1969), 58.

Chapter 5. The War Economy

1. Jean Hotz, *Handelsabteilung und Handelspolitik in der Kriegszeit 1939–1948* (Berne, 1950).

2. Ernst Feisst, *Wie hat die Schweiz ihr Kriegsernährungsproblem gelöst?* (Berne, 1945).

3. Friedrich Traugott Wahlen, *Das schweizerische Anbauwerk* (Zurich 1946).

4. Eidgenössisches Volkswirtschafts-Departement, *Die schweizerische Kriegswirtschaft* (Berne, 1950), 81.

5. Ibid., 603.

6. Ibid., 731.

7. Ibid., 133.

8. Ibid., 131.

9. Arnold Schär, *Die Fettwirtschaft der Schweiz in der Kriegszeit* (Berne, 1946), 23.

10. Eidgenössisches Volkswirtschafts-Departement, *Die schweizerische Kriegswirtschaft,* 132.

Chapter 6. A Twofold Blockade

1. Edgar Bonjour, *Geschichte der schweizerischen Neutralität* (Basel, 1970), 6:211.

2. Ibid., 6:84.

3. Ibid., 6:233.

4. Sir John Lomax, *The Diplomatic Smuggler* (London, 1965).

5. Bonjour, *Geschichte,* 6:273.

6. Ibid., 6:302.

7. Lomax, *Diplomatic Smuggler.*

8. Dean Acheson, *Present at the Creation: My Years in the State Department* (New York, 1969), 59.

9. Bonjour, *Geschichte,* 6:357.

10. Walter Stucki, *Von Pétain zur Vierten Republik* (Berne, 1947).

11. Bernard Barbey, *P. C. du Général: Journal du chef de l'état major particulier du Général Guisan 1940–1945* (Neuchâtel, 1948), 261.

12. Report of the Federal Council, June 14, 1946 (Berne, 1946), Bundesblatt 2:714.

13. Bonjour, *Geschichte,* 6:383.

14. Ibid., 6:381.

Chapter 7. Spies in the Fortress

1. General Henri Guisan, *Bericht an die Bundesversammlung über den Aktivdienst 1939–1945* (Berne, 1946), Annex II.

2. Allen W. Dulles, *Germany's Underground* (New York, 1947), xi.

3. Jon Kimche, *General Guisans Zweifrontenkrieg* (Frankfurt, 1967), 138.

4. Edgar Bonjour, *Geschichte der schweizerischen Neutralität* (Basel, 1970), 5:91 ff.

5. Hans Rudolf Kurz, *Die Schweiz in der Planung der kriegführenden Mächte während des zweiten Weltkrieges* (Biel, 1957), 17.

6. Kimche, *General Guisans Zweifrontenkrieg,* 156.

7. Guisan, *Bericht an die Bundesversammlung,* 52.

8. Bonjour, *Geschichte,* 4:469.

9. Jakob Huber, *Bericht des Chefs des Generalstabs an den Ober-*

befehlshaber der Armee über den Aktivdienst 1939–1945 (Berne, 1946), 514.

10. Guisan, *Bericht an die Bundesversammlung,* Annex II.

11. Huber, *Bericht des Chefs des Generalstabs,* 513.

12. Bonjour, *Geschichte,* 4:473.

Chapter 8. A Country's Privilege and Burden

1. Edgar Bonjour, *Geschichte der schweizerischen Neutralität* (Basel, 1970), 4:23.

2. Fred Luchsinger, *Die Neue Zürcher Zeitung im Zeitalter des zweiten Weltkrieges 1930–1955* (Zurich, 1955), 215 ff.

3. Bernard Barbey, *P. C. du Général: Journal du chef de l'état major particulier du Général Guisan 1940–1945* (Neuchâtel, 1948), 74.

4. Carl Ludwig, *Die Flüchtlingspolitik in den Jahren 1933 bis 1955* (Berne, 1957).

5. Alois Ricklin, Hans Haug, Hans C. Binswanger, eds., *Handbuch der schweizerischen Aussenpolitik* (Berne, 1975), 673.

6. *Neue Zürcher Zeitung,* September 22, 1942, No. 1503, (Zurich, 1942).

7. Bonjour, *Geschichte,* 6:35.

8. Ibid.

9. Peter Stahlberger, *Der Zürcher Verleger Emil Oprecht und die deutsche politische Emigration 1933–1945* (Zurich, 1970), 62.

10. Martin Hürlimann, *Zeitgenosse aus der Enge: Erinnerungen* (Freiburg, 1977), 370.

11. Elizabeth Wiskemann, *The Europe I Saw* (London, 1968).

Chapter 9. Stronghold of Humanity

1. Alois Ricklin, Hans Haug, Hans C. Binswanger, eds., *Handbuch der schweizerischen Aussenpolitik* (Berne, 1975), 660.

2. *Rapport du comité international de la Croix-Rouge sur son activité pendant la seconde guerre mondiale* (Geneva, 1948), 2:119.

3. Fréderic Siordet, *Inter arma caritas* (Geneva, 1947).

4. Paul Guggenheim, *Lehrbuch des Völkerrechts* (Basel, 1951), 2: 801.

5. Edgar Bonjour, *Geschichte der schweizerischen Neutralität* (Basel, 1970), 6:139.

6. *Rapport du comité international,* 1:650.

7. Ibid., 3:562.

8. Bonjour, *Geschichte,* 4:448 ff.

9. Ernst Gerber, *Im Dienste des Roten Kreuzes: Schweizer in Lazaretten der Ostfront 1941/1942* (Lucerne, 1969), 77.

Chapter 10. Negotiating Surrender in Italy

1. Edgar Bonjour, *Geschichte der schweizerischen Neutralität* (Basel, 1970), 6:125 ff.
2. Allen W. Dulles, *The Secret Surrender* (London, 1967), 18.
3. Jon Kimche, *General Guisans Zweifrontenkrieg* (Frankfurt, 1967), 184.
4. Winston S. Churchill, *The Second World War* (London, 1954), 6:387.
5. Ibid., 6:389.
6. Franklin D. Roosevelt, *The Public Papers and Addresses,* comp. Samuel I. Rosenman (New York, 1950), 13:547.
7. Bonjour, *Geschichte,* 6:117.

Chapter 11. Deterrence Achieved

1. General Henri Guisan, *Bericht an die Bundesversammlung über den Aktivdienst 1939-1945* (Berne, 1946), 41.
2. Bernard Barbey, *P. C. du Général: Journal du chef de l'état major particulier du Général Guisan 1940-1945* (Neuchâtel, 1948), 245.
3. Edgar Bonjour, *Geschichte der schweizerischen Neutralität* (Basel, 1970), 5:149.
4. Winston S. Churchill, *The Second World War* (London, 1954), 6:616.
5. Dean Acheson, *Present at the Creation: My Years in the State Department* (New York, 1969), 48.
6. Churchill, *Second World War,* 6:616.

Selected Bibliography

Hermann Böschenstein, *Vor unseren Augen 1935–1945* (Berne, 1978)
Eric Dreifuss, *Die Schweiz und das Dritte Reich* (Frauenfeld, 1971)
Arnold Jaggi, *Unser Land in der Zeit Mussolinis, Hitlers, und des Zweiten Weltkrieges* (Berne, 1978)
Hans Rudolf Kurz, *100 Jahre Schweizer Armee* (Thun, 1978)
―――――, *Die Schweiz im Zweiten Weltkrieg* (Thun, 1959)
Pierre Luciri, *Le prix de la neutralité* (Geneva, 1976)
Alphons Matt, *Zwischen allen Fronten: Der Zweite Weltkrieg aus der Sicht des Büro Ha* (Frauenfeld, 1969)
Alice Meyer, *Anpassung oder Widerstand* (Frauenfeld, 1965)
Janusz Piekalkiewicz, *Schweiz 39–45: Krieg in einem neutralen Land* (Stuttgart, 1978)

Index

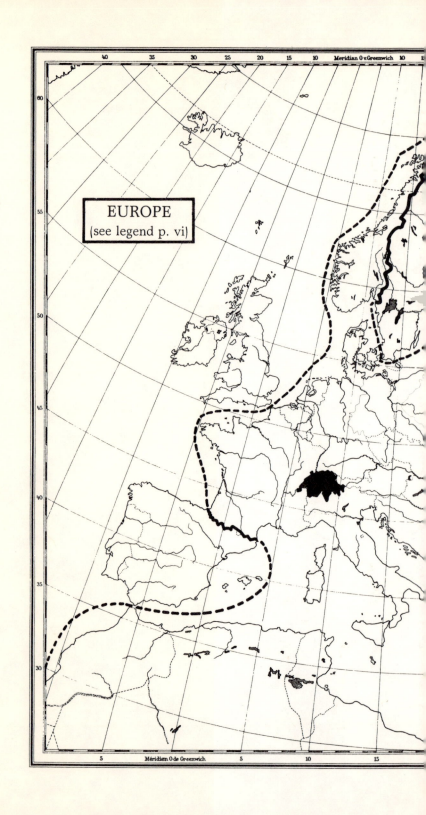

EUROPE
(see legend p. vi)